TRANSFORMING POWER OF TECHNOLOGY

TRANSFORMING POWER OF TECHNOLOGY

THE PRINTING PRESS

Samuel Willard Crompton

CHELSEA HOUSE
PUBLISHERS
A Haights Cross Communications Company

Philadelphia

Frontis: Two women set movable type for the printing press during World War I. The development of movable type revolutionized the process of printing.

CHELSEA HOUSE PUBLISHERS

VP, New Product Development Sally Cheney
Director of Production Kim Shinners
Creative Manager Takeshi Takahashi
Manufacturing Manager Diann Grasse

Staff for THE PRINTING PRESS

Executive Editor Lee Marcott
Associate Editor Kate Sullivan
Production Editor Megan Emery
Picture Researcher Amy Dunleavy
Series and Cover Designer Keith Trego
Layout 21st Century Publishing and Communications Inc.

A Haights Cross Communications ⌖ Company

http://www.chelseahouse.com

First Printing

1 3 5 7 9 8 6 4 2

Library of Congress Cataloging-in-Publication Data

Crompton, Samuel Willard.
   The printing press/by Samuel Willard Crompton.
     p. cm.—(Transforming power of technology)
Includes bibliographical references and index.
Contents: Scribes, scrolls, and parchment—Early printing—Printing and language—Printing and the religious revolution—Printing and the scientific revolution—Early American printing—The Enlightenment—Printing and human freedom—Printing and the financial revolution—Every man his own printer.
   ISBN 0-7910-7451-X
   1. Printing—History—Juvenile literature. 2. Printing—History—Origin and antecedents—Juvenile literature. 3. Printing presses—History—Juvenile literature. [1. Printing—History. 2. Printing presses—History.] I. Title. II. Series.
Z124.C76 2003
686.2'09—dc21

                                                    2003014059

Scribes, Scrolls, and Parchment

Where did writing begin?

This chapter describes the early development of writing. After beginning in the Middle East and China, writing spread to most of Europe and much of Asia by the heyday of the Roman Empire. We will discuss different types of writing and the people who performed them.

Of making many books there is no end; and much study is a weariness of the flesh.

—Ecclesiastes 12:12

Writing came first, long before printing. Writing was the major break between the Stone Age and the beginning of human civilization. The person who could write, or the tribe that had a scribe, enjoyed a great advantage over competitors.

Writing appeared in Mesopotamia (now Iraq) and Egypt around 3000 B.C. It appeared in the Indus River Valley (Pakistan and western India) around 2500 B.C., and in China a little later. This early writing was performed by scribes who labored over thick tablets; they carved the symbols of their language into clay or stone, which made the writing last a very long time. We know little about human civilizations that existed prior to those in Egypt, Mesopotamia, the Indus Valley, and China because they left no written sources. Writing and the preservation of documents are the keys to history, just as bones and ruins are the keys to archeology.

For more than 200 years, Mediterranean scholars traveled to Alexandria, Egypt, to study at the Great Library there. When it burned to the ground in 48 B.C., thousands and thousands of parchment manuscripts, which recorded much of the world's knowledge, were destroyed.

Writing continued in the same vein for more than 2,000 years. What variations there were involved the use of different types of styluses (pens) and different types of preservation material (clay, bronze, and so forth). No major change came until about 800 B.C., when the first phonetic alphabet appeared in the Western world. This alphabet came from the Phoenicians who lived in what is now Lebanon; the word "phonics" or "phonetic" comes from the Greek word "to sound."

The Phoenicians developed an alphabet of 21 letters. All were consonants; there were no vowels. The Phoenicians traded regularly with the Greeks, who were located several hundred miles to the west, and by about 800 B.C., the Greeks had begun using the Phoenician alphabet. The Greeks changed the alphabet, however, by adding vowels, and by about 600 B.C. the Greeks had developed the alphabet that is the ancestor of every alphabet in the Western world today: the phonetic alphabet of roughly 26 letters.

The alphabet is so much a part of our lives that we take it for granted, and it is difficult to think how we might behave without it. There is a case for arguing that all thinking and all production

The Diamond Sutra

Chin kang pan-jo po-lo-mi ching (the *Diamond Sutra*) is the oldest printed book that has ever been found. The *Diamond Sutra* contains a printer's statement: "Printed on May 11, 868, by Wang Chieh, for free general distribution, in order in deep reverence to perpetuate the memory of his parents." The book was printed using the wood-block method. Although slow in process, the method resulted in some beautiful productions.

Buddhism had flourished in China for several hundred years. During the T'ang dynasty, around A.D. 750, however, Buddhist texts were banned, and good Chinese were expected to read Confucian texts only. During the repression that followed, scholars apparently hid thousands of handwritten manuscripts in a series of caves in northwestern China that is now called the Cave of Ten Thousand Buddhas.

In 1907, an English archaeologist went to the caves and purchased a large series of manuscripts from the cave keeper. The manuscripts were brought to London; among them was the *Diamond Sutra*.

That the *Diamond Sutra* is in the British Museum today is a source of national anger for the Chinese people.

in the Western world today is derived from 36 characters: the letters A through Z and the numbers zero through nine. These are the building blocks of our modern world, and they are so important, so very fundamental to our civilization, that we make them child's play. But some human civilizations have not used the phonetic alphabet or the strict numerical sequence, and it has usually cost them in the long run.

No one has ever devised an instrument as clean, as purposeful, or as flexible as the 26-letter alphabet. Using sounds that correspond to letters on a page, everyone in the Western world can understand what the other person is saying, as long as each person has a dictionary and is patient with the situation. The sheer simplicity of the phonetic alphabet creates its immense power. It is indeed a transforming power, and it has affected the lives of billions of people over the last 3,000 years.

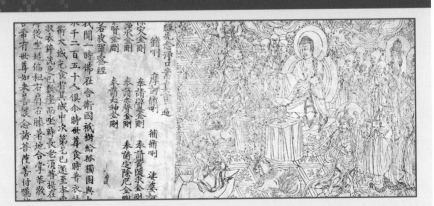

This frontispiece and text is from the oldest known printed book, which was printed in the year 868 as a tribute to the author's parents. A Chinese translation of the Buddhist *Diamond Sutra,* the book was printed using the wood-block method on a scroll more than 16 feet long. In 1907, it was discovered in a cave in northwestern China, where Chinese scholars had hidden many of the Buddhist texts banned during the Confucian T'ang Dynasty.

The Greeks used the alphabet as a vehicle for the discovery and development of their sciences, philosophy, drama, and even their politics. The Greeks did not improve on the system of writing itself; they used the same reed stylus and clay tablet that existed in the rest of the ancient world. By the time the civilization of the Greeks was giving way to that of the Romans, around 200 B.C., parchment from Egypt was beginning to replace the clay tablet. This parchment was made from animal skin, usually from calves and sheep. The use of parchment greatly increased the speed of writing, but preservation of the documents was problematic. Roll after roll of parchment scrolls piled up in the homes of Roman and Greek citizens, and the public depositories of the governments likewise overflowed. There was no remedy for the situation; the Greeks and Romans just kept on making piles of parchment.

A noble effort to preserve knowledge began in Egypt. Early in the reign of the Ptolemaic kings, around 250 B.C., a great library was built at Alexandria, which is on the western edge of the Nile Delta. Over the next two centuries, scholars from around the Mediterranean world came to Alexandria, used the great resources of the library, and added to its collections. But in 48 B.C., during Julius Caesar's battle in Alexandria with the last of the Ptolemaic kings, the great library burned. Thousands— probably hundreds of thousands—of precious documents perished that day, constituting a great loss to the ancient world.

Over the next 500 years, the book most frequently copied on parchment was the Bible. Consisting of the Old Testament and the New Testament, the Bible recorded both the story of the Hebrew people before Christ and the story of Christ's life. The first Bibles appeared about a hundred years after Christ's death and were copied throughout the Mediterranean world. At the time, many people seemed to feel that Greek and Roman learning were less important because Rome was in decline; people wanted a vision of hope for a better life after this one.

The Roman Empire staggered and fell in the fifth century A.D. For a time, writing suffered in the West. Barbarian tribesmen—Goths, Vandals, and others—sacked towns and ruined private collections, scribes declined in number, and parchment was scarce. For all these reasons, reading, writing, and the preservation of documents declined for several hundred years. But even as the West went into an intellectual eclipse, the Far East experienced a new birth of knowledge. The ideas of Confucius, the Buddha, and others had been written down around 500 B.C.; now those ideas began to spread to millions of common people. From about A.D. 400 until 1000, China and Japan were well ahead of the West in terms of the production and preservation of books and the transmission of knowledge. The only thing that China and Japan lacked was a phonetic alphabet; their languages were based on thousands of characters that took years to master. Because of this lack of a phonetic alphabet, these civilizations missed the extraordinary utility of having a simple alphabet, making both their bureaucracies and their accounting systems more difficult. When the West picked up the trail of knowledge once more, its phonetic alphabet would give it a distinct advantage.

2

Early Printing:
China, Japan, Korea,
and Germany

What does "printing" mean?

This chapter discusses the beginning of printing. A differentiation is made between wood-block printing, or engraving, and printing with the use of movable type, usually made of metal. The story takes the reader from medieval China, Japan, and Korea to Germany in the late Middle Ages. Although many people contributed in many different ways to the development of printing, Johannes Gutenberg remains the Father of Printing in the Western world.

What is printing? Where did it begin?

These questions have been debated for hundreds of years. Even in the twenty-first century, with all the methods and means available to us for printing, the basic elements of how printing came to be remain somewhat mysterious. Let us therefore start with some simple definitions.

Printing involves the duplication of written material by the use of paper, ink, and human hands (and, now, machine power). The ultimate goal of printing is to make an *exact duplicate* of the original document. As basic as this may seem, printing as defined in this way did not exist until five and a half centuries ago. In terms of time, the record of human civilization pales in the face of the unrecorded eras of humans before civilization, and likewise is the printing era quite short when compared to the length of human civilization.

Writing with a stylus began in ancient Mesopotamia and

Writing began in 3000 B.C., but for centuries there was no way to duplicate original manuscripts for distribution to interested parties. The earliest printers were thousands of scribes who simply copied original works—one letter at a time—by hand. Unfortunately, the errors that inevitably crept into the texts when they were transcribed were propagated with each new edition.

Egypt back around 3000 B.C. There was no way to easily duplicate what existed; the act of writing had to be performed time and again. The same was true during the eras of the ancient Greek and Roman civilizations; the greatest documents from Greek philosophy come to us today in a corrupted form because they were transcribed time and again, with errors creeping into each new edition. The Romans and Greeks also did not use punctuation as we know it today; they left no spaces between words and did not use capital and small (uppercase and lowercase) letters, so the documents were difficult to read. Often, they were read aloud by a scribe.

The collapse of the Roman Empire in the latter part of the fifth century brought about another crisis in the world of learning: without the stability provided by the empire, scholars and documents began to wither away. By about A.D. 600, a great many Greek and Roman documents, most written on scrolls of papyrus, had disappeared.

The classical heritage was preserved to a large extent by the efforts of thousands of scribes who worked in monasteries throughout the long period known as the Dark Ages and in the early Middle Ages. Monasteries like the ones at Iona, an island off the coast of Scotland, and Lindisfarne, an island off the coast of England, supplied the copyists who labored to save the documents of classical Greece and Rome. Beautiful manuscripts, such as the Book of Kells, revered today for their magnificent style, were made at these monasteries. But these documents were not being *duplicated;* they were slowly and painfully being *reproduced.*

Two developments, at opposite ends of the Eurasian continent, occurred in the eighth century. In Aachen, on the border between present-day Germany and France, Charles the Great (Charlemagne) brought together a number of scholars at his court. Charlemagne's scholars devised a new style of writing, one that involved the use of uppercase and lowercase letters. Called Carolingian Majuscule and Minuscule, the script made manuscripts much easier to read, and therefore to reproduce. The long, painful business of copying continued, but it was done with greater facility than before.

Eight thousand miles away, on the island of Japan in 770, the Empress Koken decreed that a Buddhist prayer be printed a million times.[1] How could this be done?

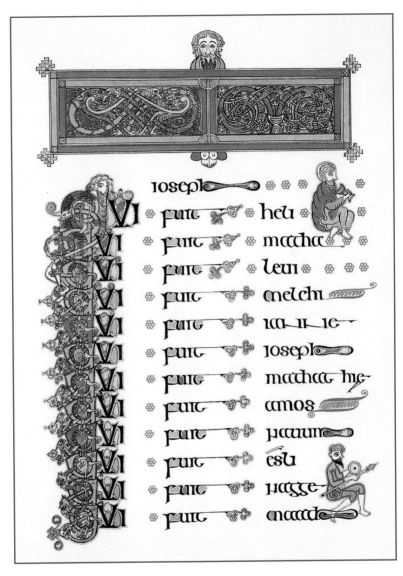

This page of the Book of Kells shows the genealogy of Christ. Written around the year 800, the beautifully designed and illustrated book was made by scribes at the monastery on Iona, an island between Ireland and Scotland. Copyists at Iona and other monasteries during the Dark Ages did much to preserve the knowledge contained in documents from classical Greece and Rome.

Wood-block printing was the answer. This meant that the writing, pictures, or both were carved into a block of wood. The printer then inked the wood block and pressed sheets of paper on top of it. This created printed pages. The two major weaknesses of the method were, first, that the pages could not be printed on both sides, and second, that making one mistake in carving the woodblock meant that the whole process had to be started over again.

The printed prayer, which was about 25 words long, was enclosed in a miniature pagoda about four inches high and then placed in houses and monasteries. This early success in woodblock printing did not continue, however, because the empress died soon afterward and her successors did not follow her lead.[2]

China took the next step forward in printing. The Chinese had led the way in the development of paper as we know it today. Both the papyrus of Roman times and the parchment or vellum used in Europe were inferior to the new paper made in China. We do not know exactly when the transfer of knowledge occurred, but historians are confident that the West learned papermaking from the Chinese.

Soon after the year A.D. 1000, a Chinese scholar used movable type for what is thought to have been the first time. Pi Sheng cut metal characters to represent Chinese symbols and printed pages in this extraordinary new way. But because the Chinese language consists of thousands of symbols rather than a few dozen phonetic letters, the new invention was not used to any great extent. Had the Chinese used a phonetic alphabet, chances are that they would have led the world in printing and consequently would have been technologically ahead of the West.

When the Mongols conquered China in the thirteenth century, they pioneered a new way of making money. Previously, wealth could only be quantified in terms of land, cattle, horses, gold, silver, and the like. The Mongols, under the Emperor Kublai Khan, were the first people to print paper money. The Venetian adventurer Marco Polo marveled at the ease with

Wood-block printing uses a design or letters carved in relief on a block of wood. The block is then inked and a sheet of paper is pressed on top of it, creating a copy of the block. In this photo, the wood block, laying flat on the open press's surface, is held in place by guides. Notice that the paper reproduction, taped to the board above the press, is a mirror image of the original design — that means that if the design were text, each letter and word cut from the block had to be backwards and upside-down.

which the Mongol lords in China printed their money and at how readily that paper currency was accepted throughout the Mongol Empire. The Western world would not print paper money until the seventeenth century (see chapter 9).

Off the northeastern corner of China lies the Korean Peninsula, and that is where the next major step in printing was taken. A new dynasty that took power in Korea in 1396 decreed that the royal government would support printing. In 1446, the Emperor Sejong announced the creation of a brand-new alphabet with 25 letters. The alphabet, which was not related to any earlier one, should have greatly enhanced the spread and use of printing in Korea. However, the emperor also decreed that printing be reserved for Confucian texts (named after the great Chinese scholar Confucius).[3] Therefore, the Korean leap forward was limited and did not transform printing. It was left to Germany, and to the city of Mainz in particular, to claim the glory for being the first to make major use of movable type.

Johannes Gutenberg was born around 1396 in Mainz. Gutenberg belonged to the patrician (aristocratic) class, and his early life was punctuated by occasionally having to leave his home, because the patrician and working classes were in severe conflict with one another in Mainz. Gutenberg moved to Strasbourg around 1420 and spent the next 25 years there. Both Strasbourg and Mainz claim to be the city where the printing press was invented, but Mainz has the stronger claim.

Gutenberg returned to Mainz around 1448 and engaged in a business arrangement with Johann Fust. The two men kept the nature of their business as secret as they could, because they were confident that they were onto something that was truly new.

That something was the use of movable type—perhaps the most revolutionary design in human history.

Until Gutenberg's time, all printing had been done with a whole page or image carved on a woodblock. But movable type changed this.

One story has it this way: Gutenberg was experimenting with making blocks of letters welded together to make words. He had come up with the idea of "movable words," but not yet with movable individual characters. One of his children suddenly burst through the door into his workshop, knocking the blocks of letters, joined together as words, to the floor. Gutenberg cursed his child's clumsiness and began to pick up the letters, which had separated from one another. As he did so, Gutenberg realized how much simpler it might be to keep all the letters separate. By so doing, he could arrange and rearrange the characters on his press and be ready to set type for a new page without having to either cut a new woodblock or permanently set the words together.

Minority Languages: Celtic and Basque

The printing press—and most forms of standardized language—are often accused of depriving the world of many of its tongues. By demanding the standard forms of English, French, or German, many dialects and subgroups have withered away.

But this has not always been the case. Take, for example, Celtic and Basque. Both languages are spoken by minority groups, and each of them may well have been *saved* by the appearance of the printing press.

In 1566, Queen Elizabeth of England commanded her master printer to cut a new set of type characters for the Celtic (or Gaelic) language. The queen wished to bring the Protestant faith to Catholic Ireland, but her innovation had a different result: the Irish became more attached than ever to their Celtic characters, which were now preserved by printing.

In northern Spain, the Basque are known as the only Europeans whose language has no connection to the family of Indo-European tongues. The Basque alphabet and language were saved for the modern world by printing, which came into that area by about 1545.

Similar works of preservation were undertaken by the operators of printing presses. The Finnish, Estonian, Latvian, and Lithuanian languages might have disappeared by now, had not the printing press arrived in time to preserve them for modernity.

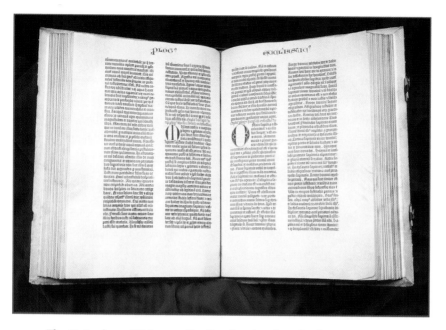

The Gutenberg Bible was the first book printed using movable type. Johannes Gutenberg originally experimented with "movable words"—blocks of letters welded together into words that could be used again and again during the setting of the text, rather than creating a wooden block for each page in a book. From that concept came Gutenberg's revolutionary idea to keep the letters separate altogether, reusing them again and again on succeeding pages.

Gutenberg was the first person in the Western world to use movable type. He appreciated the stunning power of the Western alphabet's 26 letters. Suddenly he was able to set type and print many pages, one right after another.

As is often the case with great inventors, Gutenberg did not profit very much from his revolutionary innovation.

Gutenberg and Fust fell out of favor with one another around 1454, and two years later Fust took Gutenberg to court for nonpayment of debt (Gutenberg had twice borrowed the sum of 800 guldens, a form of German currency, from Fust). The court ruled in Fust's favor, and Fust collected Gutenberg's printing apparatus.

Why then, do we all know the name Gutenberg, but few of us know the name Fust?

Just one year before he was taken to court, Gutenberg had issued the Bible that has ever since born his name. The Gutenberg Bible, printed in Mainz, was the first book in the world to come off a printing press, and it is still regarded as one of the most beautiful works ever to be printed. The two 42-line columns were a miracle of regularity and harmony, and the thick, black German letters give the Bible a great appearance of solidity and strength. All this had been accomplished through the use of paper, ink, the press itself, and the new movable type.

Although Fust and his son-in-law Peter Schoeffer became important printers, and Gutenberg's later years were spent in exile and genteel poverty, it is Gutenberg we remember. He is the person who first brought the use of movable type to Europe. He introduced movable type to a culture that could take full advantage of what it offered. Despite the charges that have been raised against him—that he was a poor businessman and that he was an opportunist—Johannes Gutenberg remains the Father of Printing for the Western world.

3

Printing and Language:
The Use of the Vernacular

AT ISSUE

What is the vernacular and what did it mean for printing?

About eight million books were printed in Europe within 50 years after the invention of the printing press. Most of the early books were printed in Latin, but an increasing number of them were printed in the vernacular, meaning the spoken language of each country: French, English, Spanish, Italian, and the like. The vernacular, for Europeans, meant almost any language other than Latin or Greek, the languages of the classical world. A new consciousness of their identity as Frenchmen, Englishmen, Spaniards, Italians, and the like began to spring up among the peoples of Europe.

A man born in 1453, the year of the fall of Constantinople, could look back from his fiftieth year on a lifetime in which about eight million books had been printed, more perhaps than all the scribes of Europe had produced since Constantine founded his city in A.D. 330.

—Elizabeth I. Eisenstein,
The Printing Revolution in Early Modern Europe

Once the power of movable type was demonstrated by Gutenberg and Fust, the use of metal characters in printing soon became widespread. Movable type soon began to revolutionize the use of different European languages.

Gutenberg and his early competitors printed in Latin, because that was the language of the educated classes of

Early movable-type printing presses used wooden and metal blocks like these to print a page of text. These presses became so popular after their invention that books began to be printed in the vernacular language of the people. Those who could not read the Latin texts of earlier books now had access, thanks to block letters like these, to the great stores of the world's knowledge in their native language.

Europe. The language's connection to the glorious days of the Roman Empire and its use in the classics written by such men as Cicero, Pliny, and Galen made it natural for elite Europeans to thrill to the Latin tongue, and for the first books to be printed in that language. But printing soon had a democratizing effect; Europeans began to want, even to demand, books printed in their own languages. This was the beginning of printing in the *vernacular,* or "native" language, meaning French, English, Spanish, German, and the like.

Printing began at Mainz, Germany, but it spread rapidly to other places. The printing press, which had taken so long to invent, was simple enough in its components that no one could patent or hold rights to it. Printing presses appeared in Strasbourg (1460), Cologne (1464), Subiaco, Italy (1465), Venice (1469), Paris (1470), Barcelona (1473), Holland (1473), Hungary (1473), England (1476), Kraków (1475), Stockholm (1483), Copenhagen (1489), Danzig (1499), Lisbon (1489), and Cagliari (1493). All together, some 252 towns and cities recorded having a printing press by 1501. Three-quarters of these books were still printed in Latin; the heyday of the vernacular tongues was yet to come.

One of the most surprising stories from early printing in Europe comes from a convent in Florence, Italy. In 1476, Fra Domenico (Brother Dominic) began printing in the convent of San Jacopo di Ripoli. Within a year or two, he had hired most of the nuns in the convent to assist him in turning out several printed titles a year. Even though this was done in a house of religion, Fra Domenico and his workers did not hesitate to print the racy writings of the Roman historian Suetonius. Neither did they shy away from the new humanist thinkers of Italy. In 1484, Fra Domenico received a commission from Marsilio Ficino to print 1,025 copies of some of the dialogues of the Greek philosopher Plato. The press managed to complete this major job in time, but the convent stopped printing soon after the death of Fra Domenico in 1484.[4]

At almost the same time, an Englishman brought printing

to his home country. William Caxton, born around 1422, may have been the single most important man in the formation of the English language. A man of business, Caxton lived for many years in Bruges, Belgium, where he learned the new art of printing. In 1472, he printed *The Recuyell of the Histories of Troy*, his English translation of a French adventure story. The book was printed in Bruges.

In 1476 Caxton returned to England. He set up shop in Westminster, on the left bank of the Thames River, very close to Westminster Abbey. In 1477 he turned out the first book printed in England, *The Dicts and Sayings of the Philosophers*. Following this introduction of the printing press to England, Caxton followed with one success after another. He printed a translation of *Le Morte d'Arthur* and brought Chaucer's *Canterbury Tales* into print for the first time. By the end of his life, Caxton had printed between 80 and 100 titles.

Besides his prolific output, Caxton also put an important stamp on the future of the English language in print. He realized that, because of the numerous dialects that existed, it was impossible to please everyone with the language used for printing books.

Caxton therefore aimed for a standard type of English, one that everyone would be able to read. Caxton set the English-speaking world on its way toward literary greatness; Shakespeare, Milton, and others would follow in his wake.

Printing continued to spread. By about 1500, Venice had become the city with the largest number of printing presses and the largest output of books per year. To no small degree, this success was due to the work of Aldus Manutius.

Manutius moved from northern Italy to Venice as a young man. Around the year 1490, Manutius set up a printing operation in that city and soon became the most successful publisher of his era. Manutius left many of the details of printing to subordinates, but he had a keen eye for business.

Prologue

Of eche of hem so as it semed me
And whyche they were and of what degre
And in what aray eke they weren ynne
And at a knyght thenne I wyl begynne

A Knyght ther was a worthy man
That fro the tyme that he first began
To ryden out / he loued chyualrye
Trouthe & honour fredom and curtesye
Ful worthy he was in hys lordis werre
And therto hadde he ryden noman ferre
And as wel in crystendom as in hethenesse
And euer honoured for hys worthynesse
At alisaundre he was whan it was wonne
Ful ofte tyme he hadde the boord begonne
A bouen alle nacions in pruce
In lettowe hadde he reysed and in Ruse

The rapidly spreading wave of print reached England in 1476, when William Caxton established the first printing press in England at Westminster. This page, from the prologue of Geoffrey Chaucer's *Canterbury Tales,* was printed by Caxton circa 1485.

He saw that the printing of classic works in Greek would find a large market, and in 1501 he brought out a Latin edition of Virgil's *Aeneid*. This was the first book ever to have italic as well as Roman letters; the reason was that Manutius found he could cram more italic letters onto one page than he could Roman ones. Thrift, arising from the desire to make a profit, led to the beginning of italicization. Because of Manutius's printing press and others, Italy dominated the market in books from about 1480 to 1520, but other countries were not far behind. France, Spain, and the Netherlands were eager to make up for lost time, and each nation made headway in the first half of the sixteenth century.

There were many French printers. Those in Paris naturally dominated the field, as the city itself did in so many aspects of French life, but for many years the small city of Lyon gave the capital city strong competition. In Paris, the leading figure was Robert Estiennes. Born in 1503, Estiennes became a printer early in life, and he had the good fortune to win the favor of King Francis I (who ruled from 1516 to 1549). King Francis was without a doubt the monarch of his time who was most interested in the arts in general and printing in particular. The king sponsored a number of Estiennes's projects and commanded that Estiennes bring a copy of each book published in Greek to be deposited in the king's library (this was the beginning of what later became the French National Library). Estiennes began the habit of numbering pages and gave keen attention to the title page. He also left an indelible mark on the French language by adding the accent marks known as "acute" and "grave."[5]

Less fortunate was Etienne Dolet. Born around the same time as Estiennes, Dolet grew up in the city of Lyon. He thrived on the commercial aspects of printing and might have led a prosperous and quiet life had he not given in to his desire to talk and write about religion. One of the first confirmed atheists of his time, Dolet was eventually arrested for sedition, condemned, and burned to death in Paris in 1546. He is still seen as a martyr to the cause of the free press, and he is the only French printer who has a statue in modern-day France.[6]

Another notable Frenchman of the sixteenth century is Nostradamus. Born in southern France in 1503, Nostradamus studied medicine at the University of Montpellier. He was a skillful doctor, but tales of his saving people from the plague

The King James Bible

In 1604, King James I brought together a group of English churchmen at Hampton Court. King James requested that they create a new English Bible, one based on the earlier work of William Tyndale and others. The scholars finished their work in 1610 and turned the results over to Robert Barker, the king's printer.

Barker had inherited his position; his father had been printer to Queen Elizabeth I. Barker invested 3,500 pounds sterling of his own money in the project and several times was heard to groan that the mighty task would devour him and his money. But in 1611, he turned out the first edition of the new Bible, known ever since as the King James Bible. It was a handsome folio product.

The Bible was a stunning success. Most people who saw or read it proclaimed it the greatest work yet accomplished in English literature. Even today, there are editors and proofreaders who claim they can tell from an author's diction whether or not he or she has ever read the King James Bible.

For the printer, however, the work was a disaster. Barker went rapidly into debt because his financial partners began to back out of the enterprise. In 1632, he printed a second edition of the Bible, which had the key word "not" missing: in the seventh commandment, which therefore read "Thou shalt commit adultery." The second printing was condemned as the "Wicked Bible" and Barker's reputation suffered accordingly. He handed over the title of King's Printer to one of his sons and went into an inglorious retirement. By the time of his death, he had been sent to the King's Bench (a special prison in London) for nonpayment of debt.

are questionable. We do know, however, that Nostradamus settled in central France in midlife and that in 1555 he brought out the first of his *Prophetes de M. Michel de Nostradamus.* Because he wrote the prophecies in groups of a hundred, they have usually been called *The Centuries.*

It is easy to poke fun at the prophecies. They are written in an obscure manner, and it is indeed possible to come up with all sorts of interpretations for each one. But this should

The King James Bible, created at the behest of England's King James I in the early 1600s and published in 1611, was in the end as disastrous for its printer as it was a glorious tribute to the king. Robert Barker, the king's printer, was ruined when the second edition was published in 1632 with a key word—*not*—missing from the seventh commandment, which therefore read "Thou shalt commit adultery."

not blind us to some of the "hits" that Nostradamus made. Here are a few of the best known:

> The Queen will be sent to death by jurors chosen by lot.[7]

and

> When the material of the bridge is completed,
> The republic of Venice will be annoyed by Hister.[8]

and

> The assembly will go out from castel Franco.
> The ambassador not satisfied will make a schism:
> Those of the Riviera will be involved,
> And they will deny the entry to the great gulf.[9]

Despite what his critics say, Nostradamus appears to have referred to France's Queen Marie Antoinette, Adolf Hitler, and Generalissimo Francisco Franco. It is most interesting that France in Nostradamus's time did not have a jury system, to which Nostradamus referred in his prophesy. Those familiar with the Nazi strategy of World War II will recognize the Nostradamus's "great gulf" as the Mediterranean Sea, which Franco might have helped Hitler conquer, had he been so inclined.

Nostradamus published two other sets of prophecies, in 1556 and 1566. While much of the world remains skeptical of his prophetic powers, he had the good luck to appear at about the same time as the printing press, and his predictions have remained in print so that they can be verified or disproved.

When it came to printing, Spain lagged considerably behind France and Italy. There were printing presses in Spain as early as 1475, but Spain under Ferdinand and Isabella was not given freedom of the press. Few Spanish literary figures emerged in the early sixteenth century, and even the explorations of Columbus

Aldus Manutius set up a press in Venice, Italy, around 1490. A shrewd businessman, Manutius discovered that more letters would fit on a page when they were set in italic type, as opposed to the usual Roman, and his firm's reproduction of Virgil's *Aeneid* was the first off the presses to include both kinds of type. As these pages from Horace's *Works*, printed by Manutius in 1501, clearly show, the combination of italic and Roman text made for beautiful as well as space-efficient pages.

were probably written about more extensively in other countries than in Spain itself. A telling example arose in 1525, when Simon de Collines, who was connected with the Estiennes family, printed Antonio Pigafetta's *Le Voyage et Navigation faict par les Espaignolz es Isles de Mollucques (The Voyage and Navigation Made by the Spaniards to the Moluccan Islands)* in Paris.[10] Surely it is significant that the story of the great journey of

Ferdinand Magellan was published in France before it was in Portugal (the country of Magellan's birth) or Spain (the country that sponsored his voyage).

Spanish literature did not come into its own until 1605, the year the first half of Miguel de Cervantes Saavedra's *Don Quixote de la Mancha* was published. Juan de la Cuesta printed the book in Madrid. Within months, everyone in Spain knew of the characters Don Quixote and Sancho Panza, and within the next few years the book's fame spread all across Europe. Possibly among the 10 or 12 most influential books of all time, *Don Quixote* remains a classic of Spanish literature, and a milestone of the transition out of the Middle Ages into the "modern" world of the seventh century.

Both Russia and Iceland, located to the west and east, respectively, of European civilization, obtained the printing press early on, but it was received in distinctly different fashions.

Russia, at that time under the rule of Czar Ivan the Terrible, was beginning its rise to power and greatness. Ivan allowed a group of foreigners to bring the first printing press to Moscow, and in 1564 *The Acts of the Apostles* became the first book printed in Russia. Just one year later, Ivan allowed a mob to burn the press and drive the foreigners away to appease Slavophiles who detested new things from abroad. For the next century, the only printing press in the entire country was one operated by the Greek Orthodox Church. Russian printing did not really take off until the reign of Czar Peter the Great, between 1682 and 1725.

In Iceland, however, the press was welcomed. Jon Jonsson printed the first Icelandic book at Holar in 1578, *Logbok Islendingia, hueria saman hefur stt Magnus Noregs Knogr* (a biography of King Magnus VII). The first Bible was printed in Iceland in 1584, and a number of other publications followed.

As the sixteenth century gave way to the seventeenth, a virtual babel of tongues appeared in print. Just a hundred years earlier, an educated man who knew Latin could read all the classics. Now, it was necessary to be able to read French, English, Spanish, Italian, German, and Hungarian, among other languages.

There had been a revolution in religion as well, a revolution that saw the establishment of a number of different faiths where once there had been only the Catholic (Universal) Church.

4

Printing and the Religious Revolution

How did printing change the religious life of Europeans?

In 1500, fifty years after the printing press was introduced, 95 percent of Europeans were Roman Catholic and 5 percent were Jewish. By 1600, Europeans were Roman Catholic, Lutheran, Calvinist, Zwinglian, Anabaptist, and other faiths.

Printing helped spread the words of such men as Martin Luther, William Tyndale, and John Calvin. In so doing, the printing press accelerated the course of the religious fragmentation that characterized the sixteenth century.

Here I stand. I can do no other.

—Martin Luther, 1521

A religious revolution took place in the first half of the sixteenth century: the Protestant Reformation.

The word "protestant" means "one who protests." Many people protested the abuses rampant within the Roman Catholic Church, but here we will discuss Luther, Tyndale, and Calvin.

The Protestant Reformation began on October 31, 1517, when Martin Luther nailed a few sheets of paper to a church door in Wittenberg, Germany. Handwritten on the sheets were the Ninety-Five Theses, famous ever since as the words that sparked the Reformation.

Luther, an Augustinian friar in Wittenberg, was outraged by the sale of "indulgences" by a Dominican friar named John Tetzel. Sometime in the thirteenth century, the Roman Catholic Church

Between 1522 and 1534, Martin Luther became the first person to translate both the Old and New Testaments from Latin into German so that common people could read the Bible for themselves. This richly colored illustration from the first edition of what came to be called the Luther Bible shows Babylon burning.

had decreed that the good deeds of Christ, his Apostles, and the saints had all contributed to a "Treasury of Merits" in Heaven. This treasury could be drawn upon by the pope to issue indulgences. Handwritten at first (later they were printed), the indulgences proclaimed that the purchaser had relieved his deceased parents or relatives from time in Purgatory—the way station between Heaven and Hell. People knew—at least at first—that even indulgences could not ensure anyone's salvation, and that they had to be purchased for someone else, not for oneself.

Centuries passed and the sale of indulgences continued. In around 1515, Pope Leo X struck a bargain with Archbishop Albert of Magdeburg, Germany. Albert borrowed 10,000 gold ducats (a unit of currency) from the Fugger family of German bankers and sent the money to Rome so that the pope could continue building St. Peter's Basilica. Albert was granted a papal dispensation to hold three archbishoprics at the same time, making him the most powerful church official in Germany. Albert needed to repay the Fuggers, of course, so the pope granted him a seven-year monopoly on the sale of indulgences within Germany.

Albert hired Friar John Tetzel to sell indulgences in northern Germany. Tetzel was unscrupulous; he led people to believe that the purchase of indulgences could pardon their parents or relatives from any and all sins they might ever have committed. This was, of course, a lie.

Learning of the deception, Luther penned his Ninety-Five Theses and posted them on the church door. They begin:

> In the desire and with the purpose of elucidating the truth, a disputation will be held on the underwritten propositions at Wittenberg, under the presidency of the Reverend Father Martin Luther, Monk of the Order of St. Augustine, Master of Arts and of Sacred Theology, and ordinary Reader of the same in that place. He therefore asks those who cannot be present and discuss the subject with us orally, to do so by letter in their absence. In the name of our Lord Jesus Christ. Amen.
>
> 1. Our Lord and Master Jesus Christ in saying "Repent ye," etc., intended that the whole life of believers should be penitence.
>
> 2. This word cannot be understood of sacramental penance, that is, of the confession and satisfaction which are performed under the ministry of priests.[11]

Luther went on to say that the pope had no authority to pardon sins, only God could do so. The Reformation had begun.

Though Luther had intended to create only a serious, scholarly debate, the theses were swiftly printed and distributed by Hans Lufft of Wittenberg.[12] All of Germany heard about the theses within a month, and all of Europe learned of it within the next three months.

The Koran in Print

The Koran contains the verses spoken by the Prophet Muhammad between about A.D. 610 and 632. Muslims believe the verses were divinely inspired, and there are those who say that the words of the Koran, when spoken or sung aloud, produce the greatest feeling that can be imagined.

The Muslim world did not take to printing. Just as Muslims took literally the commandment that "there shall be no graven image" of God, so it also seemed sacrilegious to put the words of God into print. Therefore it remained to the printer Johannes Oporinus of Basel, Switzerland, to render the first Koran in print.

Oporinus was a professor at a university at Basel. Around 1540, he accepted the challenge to put the Koran in printed form. There were numerous protests from the people of Basel and the pope but Oporinus continued in his work. Martin Luther presented his reasons for supporting the publication in his preface to the book:

> In this age of ours how many varied enemies have we already seen? Papist defenders of idolatry, the Jews, the multifarious monstrosities of the Anabapists, Servetus, and others. Let us now prepare ourselves against Muhammad. But what can we say about matters that are still outside our knowledge? Therefore, it is of value for the learned to read the writings of the enemy in order to refute them more keenly, to cut them to pieces and to overturn them.

Oporinus brought out the Koran in 1542. The city council of Basel at first confiscated all the material, but then relented on the condition that it be sold in other cities, not in Basel. One year later, Oporinus printed Andreas Vesalius's book on human anatomy. Few printers, even in the sixteenth century, could claim to have as much diverse knowledge and interest in furthering the boundaries of that knowledge as Oporinus did.

Luther never meant to harm the Roman Catholic Church. He loved the church; it was his entire life. But he did want to reform it to prevent abuses by men such as Archbishop Albert and John Tetzel.

Just one century earlier, many Germans might have dismissed Luther as a crank. But the growing number of printing presses had increased the number of Bibles in existence. Granted, most of those Bibles were in Latin, and few ordinary people could read that language. Educated people could, however, and they often spread their own interpretation of the word of God. Without intending to, Luther had started a spiritual revolution.

But Pope Leo X had other ideas on the matter. To him, the rebuilding of St. Peter's Basilica was the primary concern. Second to that was the matter of obedience: the pope would not allow a German monk to tell him he must reform the church. So Pope Leo sent a papal bull (an order) to Luther commanding him to retract his statements and renounce his beliefs.

Luther publicly burned the letter.

Two years later, in 1521, the German Emperor Charles V convened a council at the city of Worms. The emperor presided while Luther and papal representatives argued for hours over the matters of indulgences and the obedience required by a monk to the pope. Finally, Luther stated flatly: "Here I stand. I can do no other."

Luther meant that his own understanding of the Bible, informed by years of study, had led him to believe that the pope and cardinals were wrong. The church must be reformed, he said.

Emperor Charles V pronounced Luther an outlaw and decreed that no man should shelter him. But the dukes and counts in the northern part of Germany sheltered Luther for their own reasons: they wanted to use him as a pawn in their fight against imperial authority. Luther, as usual, was no man's pawn; he had his own plans.

In 1522, Luther translated the Bible from Latin to German. This was the first time that the New Testament had been translated into the vernacular.

The Bible was soon printed and became one of the first true bestsellers of the day. Luther's great accomplishment was having translated the Bible into the High German of the period, which became the basis for the modern German language. More than that, Luther had suddenly empowered thousands, if not millions, of people who wanted to read the Bible for themselves. And most of this had been accomplished through the use of the printing press.

Luther had done his major work. Although he lived another 25 years and was the emblem of the Protestant Reformation, his major efforts were completed. Other Protestants came forward to take up the banner.

William Tyndale was born around 1494 in Gloucestershire, England. From an early age, he was inspired by the new art of printing, and he believed it was his duty to use that art to spread the word of God. After graduating from Cambridge University, Tyndale went to Belgium, where he spent several years translating the New Testament into English.

King Henry VIII, who had not yet become the religious rebel who would found his own church, was not pleased with Tyndale's intention to expose ordinary people to the Bible. English agents went to Belgium to track down Tyndale, but it was too late; Tyndale's work was printed in eight volumes in Antwerp in 1525. Although the book was banned in England, hundreds of copies were smuggled into the country and provided a starting point for a new Protestant Reformation there. Tyndale was hunted down by both English agents and agents of Emperor Charles V; he was found in 1535 and convicted of heresy and executed in 1536. His last words were, "Lord, open the King of England's eyes." [13]

As it turned out, in 1536 King Henry VIII had come to a new resolution concerning religion, but most scholars agree it was

William Tyndale translated the New Testament into English, much to the dismay of England's King Henry VIII, who didn't want his subjects to be able to read the Bible for themselves. Nonetheless, Tyndale's translation was published in eight volumes in 1525. The title page and Tyndale's portrait on the frontispiece of the New Testament are shown here.

due to the Roman Catholic Church's laws on marriage, divorce, and the question of succession to the throne. After 20 years of marriage to Catherine of Aragon, Henry had one daughter, Mary, but no son to succeed him on the throne. He wanted to divorce Catherine, but could not because he had received a papal dispensation to marry her in the first place (because she was the widow of Henry's brother, Arthur).

Frustrated by the refusal of Pope Clement VII to grant the divorce and by other longstanding conflicts with the Roman

Catholic Church, Henry announced that he would create his own church. The Church of England, an Anglican faith, was very much based on the Catholic model, but the king or queen of England was, and still is, the head of the church as well as sovereign of the nation.

Henry created a new church, but it was left to Thomas Cranmer, the archbishop of Canterbury, to create a new prayer book. Edward Whitechurch printed the *Book of Common Prayer* in London in 1549, two years after Henry's death; by then, Henry's son Edward, from Henry's third marriage, had taken the throne. The *Book of Common Prayer* became a regular feature of English life. When King Edward died in 1553, his older half sister, Mary, the daughter of Catherine of Aragon, succeeded him. Queen Mary attempted to turn the nation back to Roman Catholicism. She had nearly 300 prominent churchmen burned at the stake because they would not abjure, or renounce, the *Book of Common Prayer*. The printers of the book, Whitechurch among them, escaped this fate, perhaps because Queen Mary thought them unimportant compared to the church officials.

The English Reformation came to an uneasy close when Elizabeth I took the throne in 1558. Queen Elizabeth was much wiser than her father, half brother, and half sister. She announced she would not make "windows into men's souls" and allowed her Protestant and Catholic subjects to live together in peace. The Elizabethan Settlement, as it was called, lasted for the rest of the century, but many of the English believed neither King Henry VIII nor Thomas Cranmer had gone far enough. They wanted a type of Protestantism that did not even resemble the Roman Catholic Church—and they found it in the writings of the Frenchman John Calvin.

Born in France in 1509, Calvin grew up with the writings of Martin Luther. Calvin trained for the law, but was irresistibly drawn to religion and, in 1536, his masterwork was printed by Thomas Platterus and Balthasar Lasius in Basel, Switzerland.

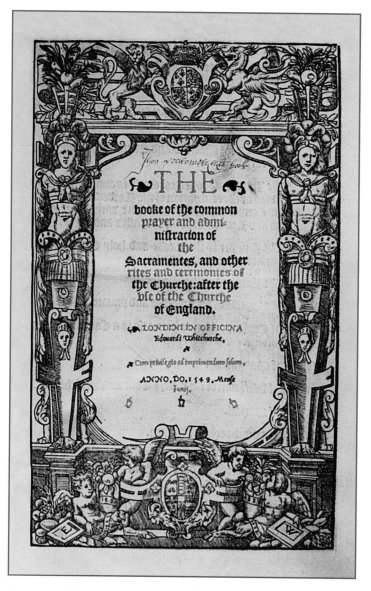

The Book of Common Prayer, compiled by Thomas Cranmer, the archbishop of Canterbury, was the prayer book of King Henry VIII's new Church of England. Printed in 1549 in London by Edward Whitechurch, the book was a regular feature in the lives of common Englishmen.

Calvin's *Institutio Christianae Religionis (The Institutes of the Christian Religion)* followed much of what Luther had taught, but went further: Calvin asserted God's omnipotence and omniscience, meaning that God was all-powerful and all-knowing. He even went so far as to say that God had already determined whether each soul would go to Heaven or Hell; this doctrine became known as predestination.

Rather than discouraging people from living pious and upright lives, the Calvinist doctrine encouraged them to demonstrate their goodness through their works in the world. Many Englishmen and -women read the works of John Calvin, and some of them became the first Pilgrims and Puritans who crossed the Atlantic in 1620 and 1630 to found the early settlements in the New World.

It might seem as though printing in the sixteenth century was all about promoting openness and new ideas. However, there was a countertrend, known to us today as the Catholic Counter-Reformation. From the pontificates of Pope Paul III through Pope Gregory VII, there was a profound movement toward reform in the Catholic Church, although it still insisted on the pope's retaining power and authority over the church. In 1559, the *Index Librorum Prohibitorum (Index of Prohibited Books)* was published in Rome.[14] The printer, Antonio Blado, had already printed Machiavelli's *Il Principe (The Prince)* and the *Exercitia Spiritualia (Spiritual Exercises)* of Ignatius of Loyola. Because the art of printing had developed into a science and thousands of books were being printed, the papacy created a list of books that Catholics should not read. Some of the greatest works of the next few centuries would be off-limits to Catholic readers.

5

Printing and the Scientific Revolution

AT ISSUE

How did printing advance—or hinder—changes in science and the scientific method?

In 1543, two powerful and important books were published. Copernicus's book on astronomy and Vesalius's book on anatomy mark the beginning of the scientific revolution, which has influenced Western civilization ever since.

From Copernicus and Vesalius to Galileo and William Harvey, from Isaac Newton to Gottfried Wilhelm von Leibniz, this chapter shows the power of the printed word in the development of modern science. Had there not been a printing press, would we understand ourselves and our world the way we do today?

> *One will be convinced that the sun itself*
> *occupies the center of the universe.*
>
> —Nicolaus Copernicus, 1543

Although there were numerous thinkers, writers, and printers involved in the scientific revolution, historians generally trace the primary line of succession as follows: Copernicus, Vesalius, Brahe, Kepler, Galileo, Harvey, and Newton.

Twenty-six years after Luther placed the Ninety-Five Theses on the church door at Wittenberg, the printing press of Johannes Petreius in Nuremberg, Germany, turned out the first copies of *De Revolutionibus Orbium Coelestium (On the Revolutions of the Heavenly Spheres)*. The book was published in 1543, the year of

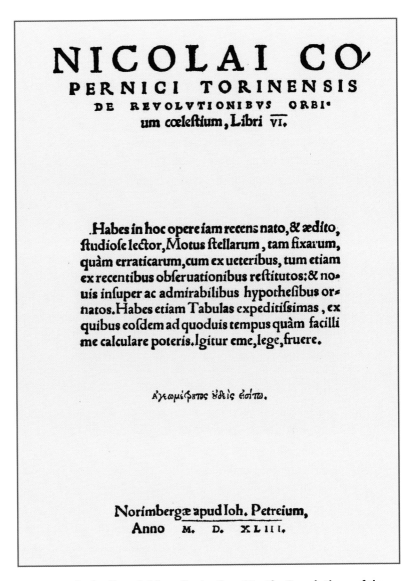

NICOLAI CO
PERNICI TORINENSIS
DE REVOLVTIONIBVS ORBI‑
um cœleſtium, Libri VI.

.Habes in hoc opere iam recens nato, & ædíto,
ſtudioſe lector, Motus ſtellarum , tam fixarum,
quàm erraticarum, cum ex ueteribus, tum etiam
ex recentibus obſeruationibus reſtitutos:& no‑
uis inſuper ac admirabilibus hypotheſibus or‑
natos. Habes etiam Tabulas expeditiſsimas , ex
quibus eoſdem ad quoduis tempus quàm facilli
me calculare poteris. Igitur eme, lege, fruere.

Ἀγεωμέφητος ὐδεὶς ἐσίτω.

Norimbergæ apud Ioh. Petreium,
Anno M. D. XLIII.

In *De Revolutionibus Orbium Coelestium* (*On the Revolutions of the
Heavenly Spheres*), Nicolaus Copernicus stated for the first time in
history that the Sun, not the Earth, was the center of the Universe.
Published in 1543 by Johannes Petreius in Nuremberg, Germany,
the theories put forth in Copernicus's book were contrary to those
of the previous 2,000 years of scientific inquiry.

the death of Nicolaus Copernicus. In the first chapter, Copernicus, a monk and church proctor, asserted that:

> First of all we assert that the universe is spherical; partly because this form, being a complete whole, needing no joints, is the most perfect of all; partly because it constitutes the most spacious form, which is thus best suited to contain and retain all things, or also because all discrete parts of the world, I mean the sun, the moon and the planets, appear as spheres.[15]

Copernicus went on to relate in great detail the beliefs of the ancient Greek and Roman scientists. They had believed that the Earth was the center of the universe, and that all other planetary bodies revolved around it. This belief had predominated since the time of the great astronomer Ptolemy (around A.D. 100), but Copernicus refuted the models of Ptolemy and all the others who had followed in his wake. In the ninth chapter, Copernicus concluded that:

> Finally, one will be convinced that the sun itself occupies the center of the universe. And all this is taught us by the law of sequence in which things follow one upon another and the harmony of the universe; that is, if we only (so to speak) look at the matter with both eyes.[16]

Copernicus had turned 2,000 years of scientific inquiry on its head. He had placed the Sun, rather than the Earth, at the center of the universe. In so doing, he forced millions of Europeans to change their views about themselves and the universe, and his discoveries continue to affect the world today.

How much did the printing press help Copernicus's ideas to gain acceptance?

The answer in this case is even more certain than in that of Luther. Without the printing press, Copernicus would have been a monk of good repute whose strange ideas might have been known to his immediate circle of friends. It is highly unlikely that his ideas would have spread to the rest of Europe over the next 100 years, or that today we would speak of the "Age of Copernicus" or the "Copernican Revolution."

But we do. We live in a world that has been fundamentally altered by the views of Nicolaus Copernicus and Martin Luther. These two men—who did not know each other—paved the way for the revolutions in cosmology and spirituality that helped to bring about our "modern" world. And they disseminated their brilliant work with the invaluable aid of the printing press.

Just three months after Copernicus's death in May 1543, another major work appeared, courtesy of the printing press. This was Andreas Vesalius's *De Humani Corporis Fabrica (On the Fabric of the Human Body)*. Handsomely illustrated by painters from the school of the Italian artist Titian, the book was printed in Basel, Switzerland, by Johannes Oporinus (the man who had printed the Koran in 1542). The volume was as remarkable to those who saw it as Copernicus's theory had been.

Vesalius undid the view of the human body that had existed since the time of the Roman scientist Galen. Galen's anatomical studies had been limited to the dissection of animals and limited exploration as a surgeon, and much of his analysis of the human body was therefore flawed. Vesalius's text described many of the functions of the human body while the drawings created a stunning image of veins, capillaries, bones, tissues, tendons, and muscles. Vesalius's work, based on dissections of humans, was the most important work in human anatomical studies for the next 200 years.[17]

The works of Copernicus and Vesalius were not seen as threats by the Roman Catholic Church—at least not at first. But as the years passed, and as one astronomer after another began to follow in the footsteps of Copernicus, the church hardened its positions on the matters of the Earth and the Sun. Was not the Earth the densest and heaviest of all planetary objects? Did not the angels live in the stars and the Moon? The debate continued

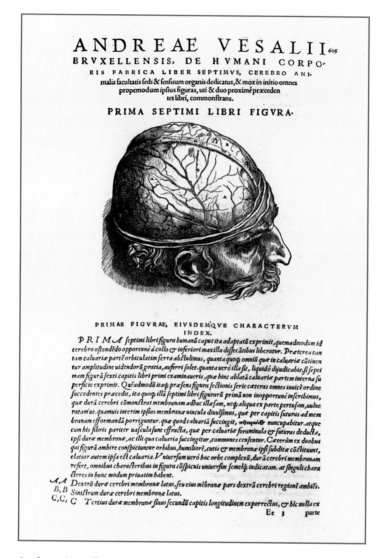

Andreas Vesalius's *De Humani Corporis Fabrica* (*On the Fabric of the Human Body*), printed in 1543 in Basel, Switzerland, by Johannes Oporinus, had as revolutionary an effect on the field of human anatomy and physiology as Copernicus's *Revolutionibus* had on astronomy and philosophy. Detailed drawings, such as this one showing the head and brain, vividly illustrated the descriptions in Vesalius's text of how the body functions.

through the researches of Johannes Kepler, a German, and Tycho Brahe, a Dane. But the crowning glory for scientific achievement in this area belonged to Galileo Galilei, an Italian astronomer.

Galileo lived in Venice. Upon his first use of a telescope, in 1609, he observed that the surfaces of the Moon and other planets were full of irregularities and imperfections and they did not fit the smooth, harmonious ideal that had been attributed to them. Galileo published his results in *Sidereus Nuncius (The Starry Messenger)* printed by Thomas Baglionus in Venice in 1610.

Galileo was at first applauded for his work. The University of Venice doubled his salary after he demonstrated that a new telescope he had designed could have important ramifications for military purposes. As the years passed, however, Galileo came more and more under suspicion by the Roman Catholic Church. In 1632, Giovanni Batista Landini printed Galileo's *Dialogo sopra i Due Massimi Sistemi del Mondo (Dialogue Concerning the Two Chief Systems of the World)*. In this work, Galileo demonstrated the superiority of the Copernican belief that the Sun was at the center of the universe and poked fun at those who still believed in the old Ptolemaic system, which held that the cosmos centered on the Earth.

One year later, in 1633, Galileo's opponents brought him before the Roman Inquisition. He was forced to abjure his declaration in favor of the Copernican system, although some witnesses swore that he muttered *"eppur si muove"* ("all the same it does move"). Galileo spent the rest of his life under house arrest by the Inquisition. But still his discoveries were published across Europe, and for the next 300 years, the church was seen as the enemy of scientific advancement and bore many sharp words from the tongues, pens, and printing presses of those who turned against the Catholic Church.

Meanwhile, medical science had continued to advance. A major breakthrough came with the publication of William Harvey's *Exercitatio Anatomica de Motu Cordis et Sanguinis in*

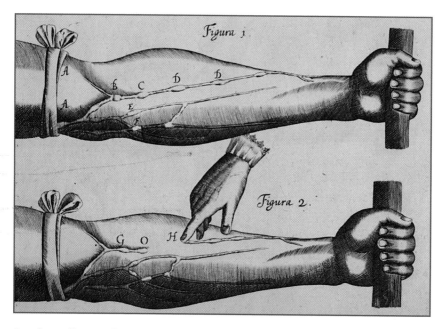

Another milestone in medical publishing was reached in 1628 with the printing of William Harvey's *Exercitatio Anatomica de Motu Cordis et Sanguinis in Animalibus (Anatomical Studies on the Motion of the Heart and Blood in Animals)* by the press of William Fitzer in Frankfurt, Germany. Harvey's book tracked the course of blood through the arteries, capillaries, and veins of the human body, as this illustration from the book shows.

Animalibus (Anatomical Studies on the Motion of the Heart and Blood in Animals). Printed by William Fitzer in Frankfurt, Germany, in 1628, this book showed how the blood vessels, capillaries, and arteries work. Fitzer was an Englishman, but he found that it was cheaper to publish in Frankfurt than at home. One of the greatest books in English history was therefore published outside of the country.[18]

The crowning glories of seventeenth-century science came toward the century's end. In 1684, Christopher Gunther of Leipzig, Germany, printed Gottfried Wilhelm von Leibniz's *Nova Methodus pro Maximis et Minimis (New Method for the Greatest and the Least),* Leibniz's explanation of mathematical differential calculus. Just three years later, Joseph Streater of London printed Sir Isaac Newton's *Philosophiae Naturalis Principia Mathematica (Mathematical Principles of Natural Philosophy)* for the Royal Society. Newton demonstrated the law of gravity and explained that the universe operates on mathematical principles that can be both explained and understood.

By about 1690, a majority of well-read Europeans had been persuaded by the ideas of Copernicus, Vesalius, Galileo, Newton, and others. A scientific revolution had been accomplished through the power of individuals' ideas and the spread of those ideas by tracts and books produced with the printing press. Europe was ready for a new stage in its development that would become known as the Enlightenment (see chapter 7). First, however, we will investigate what happened with printing in the New World.

6

Early American Printing

When and where did printing develop in America? Did Americans take quickly to the printing process and its advantages?

The first printing done in the New World was in Mexico City. The Spanish presses in Mexico and then in Lima, Peru, held a virtual monopoly on American printing until the 1630s, when the Puritans settled in New England.

From the first New World press in Mexico City to the American Revolution and the printing of the Declaration of Independence, this chapter takes the reader on a journey through the early history of the United States. The chapter reveals the importance of the printed word to Americans and their ideas of liberty and equality.

These are the times that try men's souls.

—Thomas Paine, 1776

Some Americans believe that Benjamin Franklin was the first American printer, but printing had begun 100 years earlier in North America, and almost 200 years earlier in Spanish Mexico.

Juan Pablos was the first printer in Mexico. He emigrated from Spain in 1539 as the representative of the Spanish printer Juan Cromberger. Documents show that the contract drawn up between the two men was onerous in the extreme: Juan Pablos was expected to print 3,000 sheets of paper a day and would not enjoy any part of the profits until 10 years had passed. The death of Cromberger in 1540 changed this arrangement, however, and Pablos stayed on in Mexico City as the first printer in the New World.[19]

Some sources claim that St. John Climacus's *Spiritual Ladder to Ascend to Heaven* was printed in Mexico City sometime around 1535. If that is true, we do not know the name of the printer. But the first book of which we have definite proof is *Breve y mas compendiosa doctrina christiana (Brief Compendium of the Christian Doctrine)*, printed by Pablos in 1539. The second book to be printed was *Manual de adultos (Manual for Adults)*, issued in December of 1540. Pablos stayed in Mexico City for the rest of his life. When he died in 1561, his son-in-law Pedro Ocharte became the second printer in that city. In about 1584, Lima, Peru, became the second city in the New World to have a printing press. The Spanish presses of Mexico City and Lima turned out a good number of books in the sixteenth and seventeenth centuries, most of them having religious themes.

The English emigrants who crossed the Atlantic did so mainly in search of two things: money and religious freedom. In both cases, they were at least partly inspired by the printed word.

The first settlers of Jamestown, Virginia, were inspired by accounts they had read of Spanish success in Central and South America. When they arrived in North America, these colonists hoped to find gold or silver lying about. These hopes were quickly dashed, but they found other materials that could earn them money: codfish, tobacco, sugar, deerskins, and so forth.

One of those early Jamestown adventurers was Captain John Smith, best known for his relationship with Pocahontas, daughter of the Indian chief Powhatan. Smith was injured in a gunpowder explosion in 1611 and had to return to England to seek medical treatment. When he came back to the New World, it was as a sailor and mapmaker rather than as a settler. Smith mapped and charted almost the entire coast of what is now New England, and his results were printed in *A Description of New England,* printed in London in 1616. Smith later followed this with his *General Historie of Virginia, New-England, and the Summer Isles,* printed by Michael

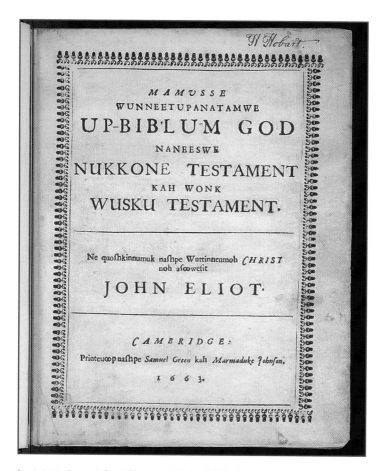

In 1661, Rev. John Eliot published *Wusku Wuttestamentum nul-lordum Jesus Christ* (*New Testament of the Lord Jesus Christ*). The book, the first translation of the New Testament into a Native American language, was printed by Marmaduke Johnson in Boston early in the history of American printing.

Sparkes in 1624. Both books were masterpieces of promotion, both for John Smith and the colonies in North America, that helped to encourage future settlers to cross the Atlantic.

In 1661, Reverend John Eliot of Massachusetts published the first Bible translated into an Indian language. His *Wusku*

Wuttestamentum nul-lordum Jesus Christ (New Testament of the Lord Jesus Christ) was printed by Marmaduke Johnson in Boston.[20]

In general, the Pilgrims and Puritans were highly literate folk. They did not publish any newspapers, however, perhaps because they saw the events of the day-to-day world as sinful or unimportant. It wasn't until 1690 that the first newspaper was published in the New World.

On September 25, 1690, Benjamin Harris of Boston printed *Publick Occurrences,* a four-page newspaper reporting the news of New England. Harris began with both a statement of intent and a disclaimer concerning news that might not be fully accurate:

> First, That Memorable Occurents of Divine Providence may not be neglected or forgotten, as they too often are. Secondly, That people everywhere may better understand the Circumstances of Publique Affairs, both abroad and at home; which may not only direct their Thoughts at all times, but at some times also to assist their Business and negotiations.
>
> Thirdly, That some thing may be done towards the Curing, or at least the Charming of that Spirit of Lying, which prevails among us, wherefore nothing shall be entered, but what we have reason to believe is true, repairing to the best foundations of our Information. And when there appears any material mistake in any thing that is collected, it shall be correct in the next.
>
> Moreover, the Publisher of these Occurrences is willing to engage, that whereas, there are many False Reports maliciously made, and spread among us, if any well minded person will be at the pains to trace any such false Report, so far as to find out and Convict the First Raiser of it, he will in this Paper (unless just Advice be given to the Contrary) expose the Name of such person, as A malicious Raiser of a False Report. It is supposed that none will dislike this Proposal, but such as intend to be guilty of so villainous a Crime.[21]

Three days later, the governor of Massachusetts and his council of advisers suppressed the newspaper. Copies were gathered up and burned, and Harris was warned not to publish the newspaper again. The citizens of Boston had to wait until 1704 for the founding of the next newspaper, the *Boston News-Letter*. The fourth newspaper in the colonies was the *New England Courant*, founded by James Franklin, Benjamin's older brother, in 1721.

It is well known that Benjamin Franklin left Boston at age 17 and went to Philadelphia, where he set himself up in the printing business. Franklin found only moderate success until the age of about 28, when he printed his first *Poor Richard's Almanack*. Let Franklin speak for himself on the means and method to which he turned:

Courteous Reader,

I might in this place attempt to gain thy Favour, by declaring that I write Almanacks with no other View than that of the publick Good; but in this I should not be sincere; and Men are now a-days too wise to be deceiv'd by Pretences how specious soever. The plain Truth of the Matter is, I am excessive poor, and my Wife, good Woman, is, I tell her, excessive proud; she cannot bear, she says, to sit spinning in her Shift of Tow, while I do nothing but gaze at the Stars; and has threatned more than once to burn all my Books and Rattling-Traps (as she calls my Instruments) if I do not make some profitable Use of them for the good of my Family. The Printer has offer'd me some considerable share of the Profits, and I have thus begun to comply with my Dame's desire.[22]

This was only the beginning. *Poor Richard's Almanack,* which combined homespun common sense with amusing verses of Franklin's poetry and news of the day, became the most popular printed matter in the 13 colonies. Franklin soon made enough money that he could go into a form of semi-retirement, from which he conducted experiments in electricity.

The Middle Colonies—New York, New Jersey, and Pennsylvania —were also the site of the most sensational court trial concerning printing. The case was the *Colony of New York vs. John Peter Zenger.*

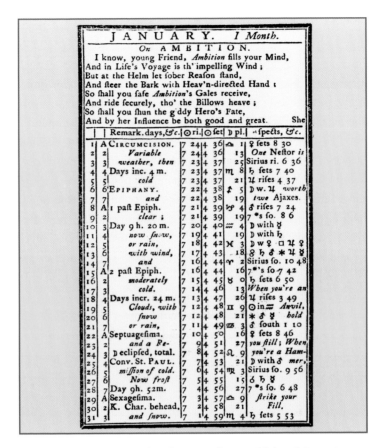

JANUARY. *I Month.*

On AMBITION.

I know, young Friend, *Ambition* fills your Mind,
And in Life's Voyage is th' impelling Wind ;
But at the Helm let ſober Reaſon ſtand,
And ſteer the Bark with Heav'n-directed Hand ;
So ſhall you ſafe *Ambition*'s Gales receive,
And ride ſecurely, tho' the Billows heave ;
So ſhall you ſhun the g'ddy Hero's Fate,
And by her Influence be both good and great. She

		Remark. days, &c.	☉ ri.	☉ ſet	☽ pl.	Aſpects, &c.
1	A	CIRCUMCISION.	7 24	4 36	♎ 1	♀ ſets 8 30
2	2	*Variable*	7 24	4 36	13	*One* Neſtor *is*
3	3	*weather, then*	7 23	4 37	25	Sirius ri. 6 36
4	4	Days inc. 4 m.	7 23	4 37	♏ 8	♄ ſets 7 40
5	5	*cold*	7 23	4 37	21	♃ riſes 4 37
6	6	EPIPHANY.	7 22	4 38	♐ 5	☽ w. ♃ *worth*
7	7	*and*	7 22	4 38	19	*two* Ajaxes.
8	A	1 paſt Epiph.	7 21	4 39	♑ 4	♂ riſes 7 24
9	2	*clear ;*	7 21	4 39	19	7 *s ſo. 8 6
10	3	Day 9 h. 20 m.	7 20	4 40	♒ 4	☽ with ☿
11	4	*now ſnow,*	7 19	4 41	19	☽ with ♄
12	5	*or rain,*	7 18	4 42	♓ 3	☽ w ♀ □ ♃ ♀
13	6	*with wind,*	7 17	4 43	18	☍ ♄ ♂ ✱ ♃ ☿
14	7	*and*	7 16	4 44	♈ 2	Sirius ſo. 10 48
15	A	2 paſt Epiph.	7 16	4 44	16	7*'s ſo 7 42
16	2	*moderately*	7 15	4 45	♉ 0	♄ ſets 6 50
17	3	*cold.*	7 14	4 46	13	*When you're an*
18	4	Days incr. 24 m.	7 13	4 47	26	♃ riſes 3 49
19	5	*Clouds, with*	7 12	4 48	♊ 9	☉ in ♒ *Anvil,*
20	6	*ſnow*	7 12	4 48	21	✱ ♂ ☿ *bold*
21	7	*or rain,*	7 11	4 49	♋ 3	♂ ſouth 1 10
22	A	Septuageſima.	7 10	4 50	16	♀ ſets 8 46
23	2	*and a Re-*	7 9	4 51	27	*you ſtill ; When*
24	3	☽ eclipſed, total.	7 8	4 52	♌ 9	*you're a Ham-*
25	4	Conv. St. PAUL.	7 7	4 53	21	☽ with ♂ *mer,*
26	5	*miſſion of cold.*	7 6	4 54	♍ 3	Sirius ſo. 9 56
27	6	*Now froſt*	7 5	4 55	15	☌ ♄ ☿
28	7	Day 9h. 52m.	7 4	4 56	27	7 *s ſo. 6 48
29	A	Sexageſima.	7 3	4 57	♎ 9	*ſtrike your*
30	2	K. Char. behead.	7 2	4 58	21	*Fill.*
31	3	*and ſnow.*	7 1	4 59	♏ 4	♄ ſets 5 53

Benjamin Franklin, under the pseudonym Richard Saunders, began publishing *Poor Richard's Almanack* with the 1733 issue. This annual compendium of weather forecasts, advice, information, and opinion was a hit with the public, with issues often selling 10,000 copies. It was published until 1757. The page shown here is from the January 1748 issue.

Zenger was born in the Palatinate country along Germany's Rhine River in 1697. He came to America in 1710 and served an apprenticeship with William Bradford, the official printer of New York City. Zenger went into business for himself, and in 1733 he began to print the *New-York Weekly Journal.*

New York politics were especially controversial at the time, and Zenger was arrested and imprisoned on November 5, 1733 on a charge of libel against Governor William Cosby. Zenger later claimed that, through the keyhole of his prison cell's door, he whispered instructions to his wife, who continued to print the *Journal* during the nine months of Zenger's imprisonment.

Zenger's friends engaged the services of the most talented lawyer in colonial America, Andrew Hamilton. In arguing the case before New York's highest court, Hamilton managed to shift the judge and jury away from convicting Zenger on what commonly had been perceived as libel; if the charges printed in the paper could be shown to be accurate, declared Hamilton, then Zenger should be freed. Despite pressure put on the judge and jury by the governor, Zenger was acquitted in 1735. This was a remarkable victory for the freedom of the press in colonial America.

Zenger went on to become the public printer for New York and then for New Jersey. Although he did not suffer the harsh fates suffered by men like William Tyndale and Etienne Dolet, he belongs among them as one who fought for the freedom of the press.

It was in Boston that American printing began, but Philadelphia, New York City, and Charleston were not far behind. By about 1750, there were nearly 20 printing presses in the American colonies turning out dozens of publications and thousands of books each year. Literacy grew apace.

English naturally dominated in the newspapers and books of the 13 colonies, but there were some interesting exceptions to the rule. Around 1743, a religious community named the Ephrata Cloister set up its press in what is now Ephrata, Pennsylvania, about 50 miles west of Philadelphia. In 1748, the Ephrata Brotherhood embarked on a very large printing venture.[23]

The *Martyr's Mirror* was published first in Dutch, then in German. At 1,200 pages, it was by far the longest publication that had appeared in the New World. The book was in great demand among the Mennonites of southeastern Pennsylvania. Later, during the American Revolution, the brotherhood printed the

Declaration of Independence in seven languages so that all Americans then in the colonies could read the statement of their freedom from Britain.

By the time the War for American Independence began in 1775, colonial Americans had one of the highest rates of literacy to be found anywhere in the world. The need for literacy was great: Americans had to be educated to help them to grasp the importance of their cause. Some of the most intriguing stories in American printing come from the fateful year of 1776, the year of American independence. Two of the men who helped to educate Americans about the cause were foreigners by birth: John Dunlap and Thomas Paine.

Dunlap was born in Strabane, County Tyrone, Ireland, in 1747 and came to Philadelphia at about the age of 10. His uncle left printing for the ministry, and by the age of 20, Dunlap had his own printing operation. He started thrice-weekly *The Pennsylvania Packet or, The General Advertiser* in November 1771, and in 1784 it became the first daily newspaper in North America. Prior to that, however, he had the honor of printing the text of the Declaration of Independence. Thomas Jefferson's text was brought to Dunlap's office on the evening of July 4, and by the next day copies were being sent by dispatch rider to all the American colonies.[24]

The American Revolution found its political voice in the printed words of an Englishman named Thomas Paine. Born in England in 1737, Paine had an extremely adventurous early life. He served on a privateer ship, worked as a corset maker, and collected taxes as an excise man in England. His fortunes hit rock bottom in 1774, and he moved to America. On the strength of a letter of introduction from Benjamin Franklin, who had known him in London, Paine soon became editor of the *Pennsylvania Magazine.* A group of friends encouraged Paine to write about the reasons for the political separation from Great Britain, and in January 1776 he published his pamphlet *Common Sense.* The first edition was anonymous, but

COMMON SENSE:

ADDRESSED TO THE

INHABITANTS

OF

A M E R I C A,

On the following interesting

S U B J E C T S.

I. Of the Origin and Design of Government in general,
with concise Remarks on the English Constitution.

II. Of Monarchy and Hereditary Succession.

III. Thoughts on the present State of American Affairs.

IV. Of the present Ability of America, with some miscellaneous
Reflections.

Written by an ENGLISHMAN.
By Thomas Paine

Man knows no Master save creating HEAVEN,
Or those whom choice and common good ordain.
                                    THOMSON.

PHILADELPHIA, Printed
And Sold by R. BELL, in Third-Street, 1776.

Common Sense, **Thomas Paine's 1776 pamphlet that set out reasons for the colonies to separate from their British rulers, was instrumental in creating the conditions for the War for American Independence. Although the first edition, published in January by R. Bell of Philadelphia, was attributed to an anonymous author, February's second edition carried Paine's name. About 150,000 copies were sold in record time.**

it was so popular that a second edition, with Paine's name on the title page, was put out in February.

Roughly 150,000 copies were sold in record time, and

Americans everywhere found new reasons to divorce themselves from King George III and England. Thomas Jefferson's Declaration of Independence remains the best-known statement of American views, but *Common Sense* was published six months earlier and perhaps persuaded more people of the need for independence than did Jefferson's document.

Paine enlisted in the American army in the summer of 1776. He witnessed the painful defeats at Manhattan and Ft. Washington, and was with General Washington when the remnants of the army retreated across the Delaware River. On December 19, 1776, at the very lowest point of the American cause, Paine printed "The American Crisis," in the *Pennsylvania Journal.* Four days later, it was reissued as a pamphlet. In it, he wrote:

> THESE are the times that try men's souls. The summer soldier and the sunshine patriot will, in this crisis, shrink from the service of their country; but he that stands it *now*, deserves the love and thanks of man and woman. Tyranny, like hell, is not easily conquered; yet we have this consolation with us, that the harder the conflict, the more glorious the triumph. What we obtain too cheap, we esteem too lightly: it is dearness only that gives every thing its value. Heaven knows how to put a proper price upon its goods; and it would be strange indeed if so celestial an article as FREEDOM should not be highly rated.[25]

Paine was with the American army when it recrossed the Delaware River and won the Battle of Trenton on December 26, 1776. The greatest crisis had been overcome.

There was a discordant voice raised in opposition to the heroics of Thomas Paine and other American patriots. In Boston, Margaret Green Draper took charge of the *Massachusetts Gazette and Boston News-Letter* on the death of her husband in 1774. For the next two years, she published and printed the paper, which, although she tried to take an even-handed approach to the war, sometimes displayed her strong Loyalist sympathies. When the

British evacuated Boston in March 1776, Draper went with them. She died in London in 1807.

The first American novels appeared during the years of the revolution. John Dunlap, who would later print the Declaration of Independence, printed Francis Hopkinson's *A Pretty Story Written in the Year of Our Lord 2774* in 1774. Isaiah Thomas of Boston brought out *The Power of Sympathy; or, The Triumph of Nature* in 1789. Susannah Rowson was perhaps the first American woman to have a novel published. Her *Charlotte* came out in Philadelphia in 1794. Rowson had settled permanently in America just one year earlier. She went on to write eight plays and a volume of verse and later to open a school for girls.

Though the American colonies had been slow to pick up the

The Declaration of Independence

The Declaration of Independence was approved on July 2, 1776, and signed on July 4 of that same year. But how did it then reach the American people?

John Dunlap was the printer for the American Congress. A handwritten copy of the declaration was rushed to his office at 48 High Street in Philadelphia. Dunlap immediately went to work, setting the document in the handsome Baskerville typeface, and was ready to print it that evening.

Within two days, copies of the declaration were reaching areas within a horseback ride of Philadelphia. George Washington had the document read aloud to the troops on July 9. Within a month, the declaration had circulated throughout the 13 colonies then in rebellion.

Sometime around July 17, Dunlap went back to the document and did a second printing, this time on vellum. Only one copy of this second edition survives today, in the American Philosophical Library in Philadelphia; in contrast, there are about 21 copies of the first printing on paper.

Dunlap, a native of County Tyrone, Ireland, went on to print the first daily newspaper in the United States. He rose in rank in the Pennsylvania militia and prospered both through printing and real estate, but nothing in his later life could equal the signal accomplishment of being the man to first print the American Declaration of Independence in 1776.

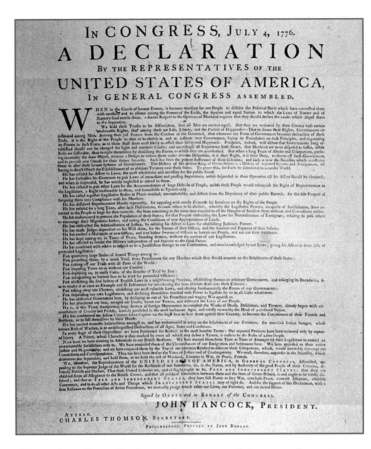

The Declaration of Independence, one of the most important documents in American history, was signed on July 4, 1776. Two days later, copies set on paper by Philadelphia printer John Dunlap took the evidence of Congress's momentous declaration to nearby towns, and within a month, copies had reached all of the 13 colonies. Twenty-one copies of this first printing still exist today.

art of printing, the country's more open social structure allowed the works of numerous people to appear in print. Next, we'll look back to the Old World during the Enlightenment, which brought a new wave of magazines, books, and newspapers to the world.

7 The Enlightenment:
Edinburgh, London, and Paris

Could the Enlightenment have occurred without printing?

London, Paris, and Edinburgh are singled out as the primary locations of the European Enlightenment. Thinkers such as John Locke and Samuel Johnson, printers such as Elizabeth Holt and William Strahan, and books such as *The Year 2440* and *The Rise and Fall of the Roman Empire* are examined.

London experienced the single greatest rise in literacy. The number of books published in London grew from 6,000 between 1620 and 1630 to 56,000 between 1780 and 1790. This represents one of the greatest leaps forward ever made in Western civilization.

He lodges at home, but he lives at the Coffee-house.
He converses more with News Papers, Gazettes and
Votes, than with his Shop Books.

—The News Monger,
An Essay in Defence of the Female Sex

An Essay in Defence of the Female Sex was published in London in 1696. Authorship of the book is still in dispute, since it was published anonymously, but it was dedicated to Anne, Princess of Denmark. The book continues as a description of men's weaknesses and the disregard that is paid to women's strengths. One of the many humorous male characters drawn is the News Monger, whom the author describes as follows:

He is one whose Brains having been once overheated, retain something of the Fire in 'em ever after. . . . He lodges at home, but he lives at the Coffee-house. He converses more with News Papers, Gazettes and Votes, than with his Shop Books, and his constant Application to the Publick takes him of all Care for his Private Concern. He is always settling the Nation, yet cou'd never manage his own Family. He is a mightly Stickler at all Elections, and tho' he has no Vote, thinks it impossible any thing shou'd go right unless he be there to Bawl for it.[26]

Written more than 300 years ago, *An Essay in Defence of the Female Sex* has a distinctly modern ring; many men and women today might recognize themselves in the descriptions in its pages. The book was published at the beginning of the intellectual phenomenon known as the European Enlightenment.

For the sake of convenience, we use the year 1690 as the beginning of the Enlightenment, the year in which John Locke's *An Essay Concerning Human Understanding* was printed in London by Elizabeth Holt. The only other thing we know about Holt is that she also printed Thomas Bray's *An Essay towards Promoting all Necessary and Useful Knowledge, both Divine and Human, in all the parts of His Majesty's Dominions, both at Home and Abroad* in 1697 for the Society for Promoting Christian Knowledge. The honor that would have accrued to the printer of John Locke's work was substantial, and indicates that Holt's position as a printer was significant. Perhaps she was the widow of a printer, or perhaps she was a very enterprising woman who made her way into the printers' ranks. In either case, her accomplishments were rare; printers remained almost exclusively male until the twentieth century.

Locke's *Essay Concerning Human Understanding* is often described as the work that provided the intellectual basis for the right of private property, for the ideas expressed in the

Declaration of Independence, and for numerous other influential ideas. Locke was one of the first philosophers to express the belief that there are no innate ideas, that all ideas are formed from experience, which begins at birth. Much of the current interest in debates such as "nature vs. nurture" derives from Locke's book.

The Enlightenment reached towns and cities all across Europe. Hungarians, Swiss, Poles, Italians, and Swedes took part in the phenomenon. But a historian forced to pin down the Enlightenment to a handful of places would most likely identify three: Edinburgh, London, and Paris.

Edinburgh was the traditional capital of the Scottish nation, but Scotland and England had joined together in an Act of Union in 1707. From then on, Edinburgh lost its political importance, although its intellectual importance soared. The Scots were not numerous as a people, but they influenced the eighteenth century to a degree disproportionate to their numbers. One major way in which they did this was through their use of the printing press.

London had long been the commercial and the political capital of England; now it was the capital for Scotland as well. Between 1700 and 1750, London began to lead in cultural affairs—print in particular—to an extent that far exceeded that of any other capital city. Some numbers help to relate the scale.

During the 1620s, about 6,000 books were printed in London. Ninety years later, from 1710 to 1720, about 21,000 titles were printed. By 1790, just three generations later, the number soared to about 56,000 titles.[27] Some famous titles published during this heyday of British printing include Daniel Defoe's *True-Born Englishman,* which came out in 1701, and *Robinson Crusoe,* published in 1719. Samuel Richardson's *Pamela,* which many critics consider the first modern novel, came out in 1740. Henry Fielding's *Tom Jones* appeared in 1749.[28]

This proliferation of books does not even include the great number of broadsides (printed sheets that were not bound) or

Literary scholars consider Samuel Richardson's _Pamela_, published in 1740, to be the first modern novel. This illustration from _Pamela_ shows a gentleman taking the title heroine by the hand.

newspapers that flourished throughout the century. In 1700, London had four newspapers: the _London Gazette_, the _Post-Boy_, the _Post-Man_, and the _Flying Post_. Nearly a dozen other newspapers followed during the eighteenth century, among them the _London Evening-Post_, the _London Journal_, and the _Daily Advertiser_. Newspapers also began to be published in the countryside.

The long career of Samuel Johnson can perhaps be used as an emblem of what London's Enlightenment was like. Born in the English Midlands in 1714, Johnson was the son of an impoverished bookseller. He went to London in 1737 and was a "hack writer," that is, someone who turned out as much copy as he could and sold it in as many places as possible. During these years of turning out this "pulp," Johnson was also working on his masterpiece, *A Dictionary of the English Language,* which was printed in 1755. The dictionary became the standard British English dictionary, as opposed to American English or Australian English. The dictionary won Johnson fame, but not much fortune; he once commented, "No one but a blockhead ever wrote for money."

Johnson's home on Fleet Street became the gathering place for a number of British writers, thinkers, and politicians. Thousands of Johnson's comments have come down to us through the written words of James Boswell. Born in Scotland, Boswell went to London to meet with Johnson, spent most of the next 20 years in the company of the great man, and preserved his sayings for us in what is considered by many to be the first great modern biography, *The Life of Doctor Johnson.*

Johnson, Boswell, and other British men of letters were astounded by the great increase in the number of printed volumes from 1770 to 1780. During the same years that the American colonists fought for their independence (whom Johnson derided by saying, "How is it that we hear the greatest yelps for liberty from those who drive Negroes?"), a handful of British authors and printers broke new ground. The most famous of the printers was William Strahan.

Born in Edinburgh in 1715, Strahan became a journeyman printer and moved to London in the 1740s. By 1770, he had become prosperous enough to purchase a share in the company that printed for the government of King George III. Strahan, who apparently was a man of considerable learning as well as an expert printer, was publisher of or helper to Samuel Johnson,

Writer Samuel Johnson compiled over a period of many years the standard dictionary of British English — *A Dictionary of the English Language* — and published it in 1755. Johnson is shown here with writers James Boswell and Oliver Goldsmith. Boswell's biography of Johnson, *The Life of Doctor Johnson*, is considered by many critics to be the first great modern biography.

Thomas Hume, Adam Smith, Edward Gibbon, William Robertson, and Sir William Blackstone.

Strahan formed a printing partnership with Thomas Cadell. Born in Bristol in 1742, Cadell later related his interest in printing to his purchase of a book for all of his three pennies when he was 14. It so caught his interest that it shaped the rest of his life.

Strahan and Cadell enjoyed a remarkably successful career, best illustrated by their output during the mid- to late 1770s. Between 1776 and 1778, they printed the six-volume *The History*

01101010 **70** THE PRINTING PRESS

of the Decline and Fall of the Roman Empire, by Edward Gibbon. The author and Cadell believed that a printing of 500 books would be sufficient, but Strahan decided to take a risk and increase the number to 1,000. Thirty-five hundred copies were soon printed and sold, and Gibbon was hailed as the genius of the day.

In 1776, Strahan and Cadell printed Adam Smith's *An Inquiry into the Nature and Causes of the Wealth of Nations.* Still considered one of the great economic texts, Smith's work made a clear case that nations should act in ways similar to those of individuals when it came to private property and the building of wealth.

One year later, in 1777, Strahan and Cadell printed Captain James Cook's *A Voyage towards the South Pole, and Round the World* in two volumes. Together, Strahan and Cadell had printed the greatest history book, the greatest study of economics, and the greatest true adventure tale of the decade.

Years later, Benjamin Franklin, then living in Paris, wrote to Strahan, "I remember your observing to me that no two journey-men printers had met with such success in the world as ourselves." [29]

The Paris that Franklin enjoyed so much was the third center of the European Enlightenment. The salons of Paris, many of them hosted by beautiful and imposing middle-aged women, were the sites of impassioned discussions of such issues as life, work, and happiness.

There was, however, much stronger censorship of the press in France. King Louis XV, who reigned from 1715 to 1774, and King Louis XVI, who reigned from 1774 to 1793, feared the power of the press and kept hundreds of censors employed. Therefore, the leaders of the French Enlightenment did some of their work in secret and printed many of their publications in Holland or Switzerland. From there, the books were smuggled back into France.

The 1750s was one of the most ambitious decades for

French printers; in fact the greatest single work of printing of that decade was undertaken at Paris by Denis Diderot and Jean Le Rond d'Alembert as editors of the famous *Encylopedie*.

The full title was *Encylopédie ou Dictionnaire raisonné des sciences, des arts et des métiers, par une Société de Gens de lettres*, and it was printed by David l'aine Briasson in Paris between 1751 and 1765. The 17 volumes contained detailed information on almost every conceivable aspect of material life; ships, houses, and factories were drawn broken into their constituent parts. The illustrations were superb, but the painstaking method of creating them ensured that the *Encyclopédie* would take a long time to be printed.

Diderot and d'Alembert made their names and fortunes on the *Encylopédie*. They were hailed as geniuses, as the most comprehensive conveyors of knowledge of their time. There was much truth to that opinion, but if only the *Encyclopédie* were consulted, the view of the French Enlightenment would be rather narrow.

Books existed in a world that was rich in voice, sound, and metaphor. The Parisians were known for their wit, and the underground writings of the French Enlightenment were received with great interest. Princeton University's Robert Darnton has identified three books that he considers to be the "best-sellers" of pre-revolutionary France. They are *L'An 2440, Anecdotes sur Mme. la Comtesse du Barry*, and *Systeme de la Nature*.

Louis-Sebastien Mercier wrote *L'An 2440 (The Year 2440)*. Printed in 1771, the book was devoured by French readers, who had until then seen almost no science fiction or futuristic study.

Mercier took the reader on a stroll through Paris in the year 2440; the narrator had gone to sleep, like Rip Van Winkle, and awakened to find that he was 700 years old! Mercier described a Paris that was neat, orderly, and had a marked lack of social distinction. Even the king went about on foot, and the few carriages that existed were for the use of elderly persons who

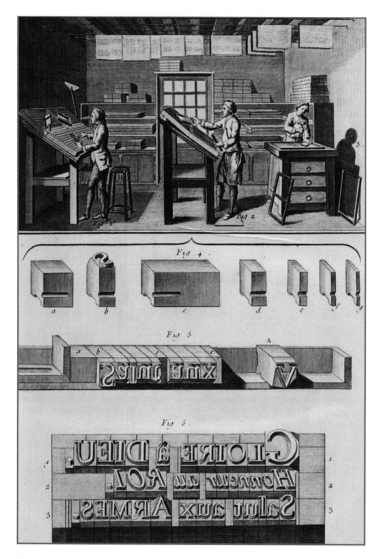

The 17-volume *Encylopédie ou Dictionnaire raisonné des sciences, des arts et des métiers, par une Société de Gens de lettres,* edited by Denis Diderot and Jean Le Rond d'Alembert and printed between 1751 and 1765 by Parisian David l'aine Briasson, detailed many aspects of the material arts. The outstanding illustrations, such as this one explaining how type is set, were instrumental to the text's descriptions of mechanical processes.

had done great good for society in their younger years. Public hospitals were open to all. Severe distinctions of wealth and poverty did not exist, and Paris seemed remarkably free of the social tensions that would be so vividly described by Charles Dickens in *A Tale of Two Cities* in 1859. Mercier created a "tale of one city," of a Paris of the future that had eliminated many, if not all, of the social abuses that existed in the year 1771.[30] Perhaps the greatest surprise of the story, however, occurred when the

Jules Verne — Paris in 1960

Louis-Sebastien Mercier looked forward to the year 2440, whereas Jules Verne looked to the year 1960.

Jules Verne is the most-read and most-translated French author of any time period. Americans today know him from his *20,000 Leagues Under the Sea, The Mysterious Island,* and, of course, *Around the World in Eighty Days.* But one of Verne's manuscripts, written in 1863, was not found and published until 1997. It did not have a title, but the translator called it *Paris in the Twentieth Century.*

Verne described his vision of Paris in 1960 and 1961, and it sounds eerily like the Paris — and nearly all the major world cities — of today. Verne describes machines that spew out money (ATMs), machines that magically produce type that has been sent from somewhere else (fax machines, print-on-demand books) and others.

But this Paris of 1960, written and described in 1863, is a Paris that has lost its soul. There is no evidence of the traditional French emphasis on good food and wine, and little of the types of parks and avenues that still give so much pleasure to the Parisian. Verne describes a soulless city in which everything beautiful and sublime has been reduced to something efficient and useful.

Fans of Jules Verne's many books claim not to be surprised at his prophecy; this, after all, was the man who described submarines before they appeared. But many an average reader who has come across *Paris in the Twentieth Century* for the first time has felt a chill run down their spine. Not only did Verne accurately predict many aspects of modern life, he also suggests that we are being propelled further and further into utilitarianism.

French author Jules Verne seemed to predict a number of aspects of modern life in his 1863 manuscript *Paris in the Twentieth Century*. This description of Paris in 1960 and 1961, discovered and published in 1997, warned of the dangers of utilitarianism.

narrator found at the royal library only four cupboards of books: one for French literature, one for English, one for Spanish, and one for Italian. Naturally, the narrator asked with astonishment what had happened to the mountains of books that had existed in 1771.

"We burned it," the librarian replies, "800,000 volumes of law, 50,000 dictionaries, 100,000 works of poetry, 1,600,000 travel books, and 1,000,000,000 novels all went up in a gigantic bonfire."[31]

Why on God's Earth would they do this? wondered the narrator. The answer came quickly: "Printing has proven to be the most important force in history, and the French protect their freedom by keeping the press entirely free. They did not burn the books because they despised them but rather because they feared their power."[32]

The reader also learned that every Frenchman of the year 2440 would write a book about what he learned in his lifetime. This book would serve as his eulogy, and then presumably be destroyed.

Even this short list of best-sellers indicates that Paris from 1750s through the 1780s was a lively, contentious place. Few readers, authors, or printers would have suspected that the revolution that began in 1789 would lead to the terrible excesses of punishment by guillotine, but then, printers, authors, and readers never have the luxury of knowing how the future will unfold.

In what ways has the printing press advanced human freedom?

"The pen is mightier than the sword," is an ancient expression. This chapter offers examples of how and when that has been the case.

Harriet Beecher Stowe's *Uncle Tom's Cabin*. Florence Nightingale's book on military medicine. Charles Darwin's *Origin of Species*. All of these books and more have helped to advance the cause of human freedom.

Critics can certainly point out cases that suggest the opposite. Adolf Hitler's *Mein Kampf* is one of the best examples. But the fact that authoritarian regimes such as Nazis in Germany needed to control the press shows that the printing press tends naturally to aid in the dissemination of knowledge, which in turn leads to emancipation far more often than repression.

The proletarians have nothing to lose but their chains. They have a world to win. Workers of the World, Unite!

—Karl Marx and Freidrich Engels,
Communist Manifesto

The Enlightenment's emphasis on rational thought led to the French Revolution of 1789. King Louis XVI and Queen Marie Antoinette lost first their power, then their thrones, and finally their lives. What began as a moderate movement toward reform became a bloody and chaotic time in which thousands of people lost their lives at the guillotine.

Welcomed at first as a sign of increasing freedom for all

the peoples of Europe, the French Revolution eventually led to a backlash by conservative writers. Even so, the output of those who were affected by the revolution is impressive.

The British philosopher Edmund Burke published his *Reflections on the Revolution in France* in 1791. Burke was no dyed-in-the-wool conservative—he had supported the arguments of the American colonists during the 1770s. But Burke was disturbed by the move toward anarchy in France. While he acknowledged that the revolution was a mighty and important event, Burke predicted that a military despot would soon lead the revolutionaries, and indeed, Napoleon appeared nine years later as if to fulfill the prediction.

Other writers, however, defended the revolution as essential to the growth of civilization. Thomas Paine, who had moved back to England in 1787, published his *Rights of Man* in 1791. Printed by the radical Joseph Johnson of London, *The Rights of Man* became an immediate best-seller. Not to be outdone by Paine, the British women's rights advocate Mary Wollstonecraft came out with *A Vindication of the Rights of Woman* in 1792; Johnson was her printer, as well. Thomas Spence published *The Rights of Infants* in 1797.

Both Paine and Wollstonecraft soon went to France, and both experienced disappointment there. Paine narrowly escaped the guillotine in 1794, and Wollstonecraft died after the birth of her daughter, Mary, who later married the poet Percy Bysshe Shelley. But these two pioneers in the cause of human freedom found many others to echo their sentiments, and their voices slowly became a powerful chorus.

Johnson continued printing controversial material. In 1798, he brought out Thomas Malthus's classic *An Essay on the Principle of Population.* Johnson was arrested in that same year for selling a pamphlet the government considered seditious. Although he was defended by the best trial lawyer of the time, Johnson was convicted and spent six months in the King's Bench, a special prison in London.[33]

Meanwhile, others advocated for an end to slavery. In England, William Wilberforce led the movement. Born in Hull, England, in 1759, Wilberforce was converted to Methodism at an early age.

Abolitionists such as William Wilberforce, seen here, used the power of the printing press to spread their message advocating an end to the slave trade. Wilberforce's *A Letter on the Abolition of the Slave Trade,* published in 1807, helped him to convince his colleagues in England's House of Commons to abolish the legal sale of humans.

This faith, which had been founded by brothers John and Charles Wesley and by George Whitefield just a few years earlier, advocated a much more visible and energetic role for church members in the world; they were to resist oppression and help those who were less fortunate. Wilberforce clearly took these lessons to heart.

Wilberforce was elected to the House of Commons (the lower house of Parliament) in 1783. Spectacularly successful at a young age and popular with all classes of society, Wilberforce nevertheless found something was missing. His diary recorded that on October 28, 1787, he had a revelation that he was to perform two tasks: to end the slave trade and to reform the morals of the English people.

Wilberforce went to work right away. In 1789, he introduced the first bill in Parliament to abolish the slave trade. The bill failed, but Wilberforce kept up the pressure; he published *A Letter on the Abolition of the Slave Trade* in 1807; the pamphlet was printed by the firm of T. Cadell and W. Davies (this Cadell was the son of the one who had earlier printed the work of so many Enlightenment thinkers). Wilberforce finally succeeded. In March 1807, the House of Commons approved his measure by the lopsided vote of 283 to 16;

Joseph Johnson: Printer, Humanitarian, Bookseller

Born near Liverpool in 1738, Joseph Johnson was raised a Baptist. He moved to London in 1754, served an apprenticeship in the printing trade, and by 1760 had his own printing press, located in the heart of the Old City of London.

Johnson became a Unitarian by 1770. As such, he felt compelled to seek out and publish authors of liberal convictions. He was the first Englishman to print a section of Benjamin Franklin's works (1780), the founder of the periodical *The Analytical Review,* and a friend and publisher to William Blake, William Cowper, and John Newton, who wrote the song "Amazing Grace."

Johnson became even more liberal, some would say radical, during the French Revolution. He published Thomas Paine, Mary Wollstonecraft, and others. He bailed Paine out of debt and saved him from debtor's jail. For this, Johnson was noticed by the British government, and in 1798 he was sentenced to six months' imprisonment at the King's Bench in London. He emerged from this experience a broken man, but his fame was undiminished. Men and women of liberal persuasions in Britain thought him the greatest hero of their time, and on his death, the poetess Maria Edgeworth wrote this eulogy:

> Wretches there are, their lucky stars who bless
> Whene'er they find a genius in distress;
> Who starve the bard, and stunt his growing Fame
> Lest they should pay the value for his name.
> But JOHNSON rais'd the drooping bard from Earth
> And fostered rising genius from his birth:
> His lib'ral spirit a *Profession* made,
> Of what with vulgar souls is vulgar Trade.

King George III gave his royal assent two days later. British participation in the slave trade ended quickly.

Wilberforce had succeeded in his first great goal. His second, to reform the morals of the English people, moved more slowly, but simply by the force of his will and success he had given "goodness" a new value among the people of his homeland. The novels of Jane Austen, published between 1808 and 1818, did much to continue this trend, and by the time Victoria became queen in 1838, the British people were ready for a virtuous monarch, policies based on morality, and a new value given to domestic propriety. The Victorian Age owed much to the efforts of William Wilberforce and Jane Austen.

In addition to improving conditions for its own people, Victorian England provided a ready place of asylum for intellectual and spiritual refugees. One of these was Karl Marx, a German who made London his home for the second half of his life.

In 1848, Karl Marx and Friedrich Engels published their *Manifest der Kommunistischen Partei (Communist Manifesto)* in London. The German printer J. E. Burghard printed 500 copies of the 21-page manifesto in pamphlet form. The manifesto was soon sent to all parts of Europe. The last words of the document are: "The proletarians have nothing to lose but their chains. They have a world to win. Workers of the World, Unite!"[34]

Marx went on to write *Das Kapital (Capital),* which was printed by Otto Meissner in Germany in 1867.

Both the *Communist Manifesto* and *Capital* argued the same point: that capitalism allowed leaders of industry to make virtual slaves of their employees. Marx was optimistic however; he believed that the workers would eventually triumph over their capitalist masters, no matter how long the struggle lasted. Marx's works were influential in starting the Communist movement and provided the theoretical basis for both the Russian Revolution of 1917 and the Chinese Communist Revolution of the 1930s. Few men have ever had such a profound influence through the power of their ideas and use of their pens.

Just four years after the appearance of the *Communist Manifesto*, an American woman issued the first great tract against slavery in her nation. True, works by William Lloyd Garrison, Frederick Douglass, and others had been printed before, but the printing of Harriet Beecher Stowe's *Uncle Tom's Cabin* turned the tide in both the United States and abroad. Printed in Boston in 1852, the publisher hoped the book would be a modest success; instead, all 10,000 copies sold out within one week, and subsequent printings sold more than 300,000 copies over the next year. This volume of sales was unprecedented, and Stowe and the plight of the slaves became known the world over.

Other landmark books followed. In 1858, a London printer brought out Florence Nightingale's *Notes on Matters Affecting the Health, Efficiency, and Hospital Administration of the British Army*. The 800-plus-page book discusses the miseries endured by the average British soldier invalid during the Crimean War. Six chapters were devoted to the history of what had been, and three other chapters were filled with recommendations for improvement. The book did not have a wide circulation, but people of influence who were responsible for setting up the new Royal Commission on the army did receive it. Nightingale had as profound an effect on the state of British army medicine as Stowe did on exposing slavery.

Before the decade was over, two more books of monumental importance were printed, both in London. In 1859, John Murray brought out Charles Darwin's *On the Origin of Species by Means of Natural Selection*, and in the same year John W. Parker printed John Stuart Mill's *On Liberty*.

The importance of these two books cannot be overstated. Darwin, who had spent four years as a natural scientist aboard HMS *Beagle*, had taken many years to refine and polish his argument. Unlike Copernicus three centuries earlier, Darwin published within his lifetime; the result was an uproar.

Darwin argued that all living organisms are in a continual state of evolution, that nothing in the natural world is the same now as it was when the Earth was created. Darwin was a Christian and it pained him to present the scientific truth in opposition to biblical lore, but his researches left no doubt that human life, like that of all the other animals, was engaged in a continual struggle for survival that forced organisms to adapt or perish. Needless to say, his theory was distinctly unpopular; critics savaged the idea, and cartoonists had a field day with Darwin's furry brow and "apelike" appearance.

John Stuart Mill's book produced much less controversy, but it was as revolutionary to society and the life of man as Darwin's great book was. Mill argued that the individual knows no bounds when it comes to his liberty and his desire for personal freedom. In addition, he said, individuals who pursued their own calling, their own destiny, were doing what was best for the community as well as themselves. The book was nothing less than a dramatic call for freedom for the individual, and Western peoples have been following Mill's doctrine since then.

About 15 years after the publication of Darwin and Mill's books, there came another step forward in the technical arena—the appearance of the typewriter. Three men from Milwaukee, Wisconsin—Christopher Latham Sholes, Carlos Glidden and S.W. Soule—designed the first typewriter in 1867 and patented it the following year. In 1874, the device was placed on the market by E. Remington & Sons of Ilion, New York.

The typewriter allowed a single person to imprint type on a page without the help of a press or any other heavy instrument. The most impressive things about the new typewriter were its light weight and portability; anyone could now put words into print without taking sheets of paper written in longhand to a printer.

The typewriter brought about the modern office worker. Until the 1870s and 1880s, the office staff of companies was kept as small as possible to keep costs down; the emphasis was on the "people in the field," whether they were surveyors or construction workers. But the invention of the typewriter meant that offices could generate extensive reports without incurring the high

The typewriter hit the market in 1874 and revolutionized not only the business world, but women's lives, as well. By 1900, large pools of women typists and secretaries were documenting the dealings of thousands of American companies and learning about the wider world at the same time. Women from that time forward would play an increasingly important role in the business world.

costs of sending the material out to printers. Therefore, the typewriter increased the number of office workers and created a whole new staff of secretaries and typists.

Most of the first typists and secretaries were men due to the belief at the time that work outside the home was the "man's job." But companies that hired female workers soon found that women made better typists and secretaries than men. Some of the difference was based on eyesight. Men tend to have better long-range vision and spatial abilities; women tend to have better sight up close and have far superior peripheral vision. These qualities made women better office workers, and by about 1900, most American companies hired more women than men for office work.

Today, many people look down on secretarial jobs, which often carry the title of "administrative assistant." But in 1900, and for the next 70 or 80 years, office jobs were a major source of a newfound freedom for American women; they experimented in the workplace, learned about the larger world, and slowly prepared to take on other functions. The women's movement of the 1960s and 1970s would have been nearly impossible without the large number of women doing office work, and many of those women got their jobs courtesy of the manual typewriter. Once again, a technology based on type provided a new route to human freedom.

Then came the Linotype machine. The word comes from "line of type."

The Linotype, first developed by Ottmar Mergenthaler, was the vehicle for the greatest revolution since the fifteenth century. Gutenberg had revolutionized the ability to print by making movable type, characters that could be positioned and repositioned on the printing board. Now, with Mergenthaler's new machine, one man could perform the work of several; he could set an entire "line of type" without touching the characters at all. Mergenthaler explained:

> The machine does away with the use of ordinary type and abolishes composition and distribution. It enables the publisher to produce for each issue new, clean type-surfaces or forms at from thirty to sixty per cent less than the cost of composition.
>
> It avoids the usual investment in type.
>
> It avoids the necessity of using old and worn faces.
>
> It permits any desired change of faces, from Agate to Small Pica.[35]

How did it do this? The Linotype machine was about seven feet high. A single person sat before a special screen that allowed him or her to compose a "line" by depressing keys to select character molds, into which molten lead alloy was poured to print

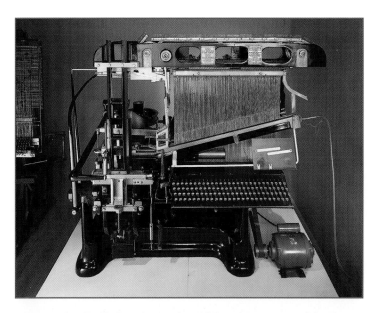

Ottmar Mergenthaler's invention of the Linotype machine in 1884 was the biggest revolution in printing since Gutenberg's movable type. The machine's operator used a typewriter keyboard to select the letters making up a "line of type." The molds of these letters were then filled with molten lead alloy that was cooled and the line was printed. The resulting impression was clean and clear, and the machine was highly efficient.

the line. Pressing a few other keys sent the character molds back to the machine, and the process began again.

Mergenthaler's estimated increase in productivity of 30 to 60 percent was too low. The Linotype machine revolutionized printing, and vast quantities of new books and newspapers were printed.

The printing press had already contributed to the spread of human freedom by reproducing calls for the emancipation of women, slaves, and workers. Then, the typewriter and the Linotype machine increased the press's impact. For those who wanted to write, publish, and influence others, the future became even more open than the previous 100 years.

9

Printing and the Financial Revolution

How did the printing press alter the financial institutions of the world?

Imagine having to carry $20,000 worth of gold with you when you go to purchase a car. Imagine the burden of having to lug around your money at all times in case you want to use it.

This chapter shows how the printing press helped to advance the flow and exchange of money around the world. We will learn about the establishment of the U.S. dollar and the background of such phrases as "In God We Trust."

In God We Trust.

—All U.S. currency and coins

Paper currency and metal coins are so much a part of our lives today that we tend to forget they are relatively recent developments. As recently as the year 1600, there was virtually no paper currency anywhere in the Western world.

The Chinese pioneered in the use of paper money in the ninth century. In the thirteenth century, the Venetian explorer Marco Polo marveled at the ease with which Kublai Khan paid his hundreds of thousands of troops with printed money.

He makes them take of the bark of a certain tree, in fact of the Mulberry Tree. . . . All these pieces of paper are issued with as much solemnity and authority as if they were of pure gold or silver; and on every piece a variety of officials, whose duty it is, have to write their names, and to put their seals. And when all is prepared duly, the chief officer deputed by the Khan smears the Seal entrusted to him with vermilion, and impresses it on the paper, so that the form of the Seal remains printed upon it in red; the Money is then authentic. Any one forging it would be punished with death. And the Khan causes every year to be made such a vast quantity of this money, which costs him nothing, that it must equal in amount all the treasure in the world.[36]

This Chinese currency was printed with woodblocks, the form of printing that had existed there for hundreds of years. But the idea did not catch on in Europe until the seventeenth century, and even then it met with a great deal of resistance.

The average person's fears about paper money were well grounded. Receiving payment in gold or silver was always preferable to printed paper money. But as the European mercantile horizon expanded and merchants found it necessary to send agents on long journeys, "bills of credit," which were not quite the same as printed money, became more and more useful. A bill of credit was more like a bank check of today than actual currency.

The American colonists were among the first to experiment with using paper money. In December 1690, the colony at Massachusetts Bay faced disaster. The expedition of soldiers they had sent aboard ships to conquer the French-Canadian town of Quebec failed, and the returning soldiers demanded their pay. Lacking silver or gold, the Massachusetts government issued the first paper money in North America. The notes, struck from a copper engraving, were a handsome beginning for paper money, but many people refused to accept them.[37]

What Massachusetts had started, other colonies repeated.

In 1690 Massachusetts became the first American colony to issue paper money. This 20-shilling note, printed by John Dunlap using the wood-block method and issued in Pennsylvania in 1777, carried the obligate seal of the Commonwealth on the front and a no-nonsense notice to counterfeiters on the back.

Nearly all of the 13 colonies printed some form of paper money between 1700 and 1775, and in the mother country of England the first notes were printed around 1729. There was still great deal of skepticism about the system, however, and it was well warranted because the spread of paper money led to a devaluation of the currency. Most of the colonies were in debt at the time of the American Revolution, when they found it even more necessary to print paper bills.

It is conceivable that the printing of paper money—done first in wood-block form and then in engraving—could have occurred without the technical innovation of the printing press. However, without the dissemination of knowledge provided by books and without competition in prices and exchange rates, it is unlikely that paper currency would have made a strong showing in Europe or America.

The American Continental Congress issued currency soon known as Continentals. As the value of these paper bills decreased, the expression "It's not worth a Continental" spread. By the time America won its independence from Britain in 1783, it was more necessary than ever for the former colonies to develop a sound financial policy. The Continental Congress approved the use of the decimal system, with one hundred pennies per dollar, in 1785.

The new United States Congress issued its first law on currency in April 1792. A mint for making coins was created, and printing presses began to strike off the first U.S. dollars.

American currency moved along, although it did not truly thrive until about 1837. In that year, President Andrew Jackson announced the end of the Bank of the United States, and determined that savings should be put instead into separate state banks. The result was considerable confusion in the U.S. currency, with different banks printing money that was valued at different rates of exchange. By about 1855, the United States was approaching financial chaos.

The Banking Act of 1857 improved the situation somewhat,

but it was not until the start of the Civil War in 1861 that American leaders realized how serious the crisis was. Salmon P. Chase, the new Secretary of the Treasury, took the lead in developing a new banking and currency-printing policy.

In July 1861, just a week before the Battle of Bull Run, Chase authorized the printing of the first bills of credit issued by the federal government to finance the Union army. These were not paper currency in the sense we use the word today; they were more like savings bonds. The crisis continued to worsen, and in the winter of 1862, Chase asked Congress to authorize the printing of "greenbacks." This was the beginning of the U.S. dollar as we know it today. There was considerable resistance in Congress, but Chase pushed the measure through by pointing out how little time was left: "It would take at least a week if the bill became law before the bills could be engraved, printed, and put into circulation."[38]

Congress gave its approval and the Legal Tender Act became law on February 25, 1862. One hundred and fifty million dollars' worth of greenbacks were quickly printed and issued.

This was not the end of the financial crisis, however. On July 11, 1862, a second Legal Tender Act was passed by Congress, and a third was passed in 1863. The crowning glory of Chase's work came in April 1864, when, on his initiative, the country's legal tender started to carry the words "In God We Trust." Printers and engravers were permitted to try other slogans at their own discretion as well, but in 1955 Congress passed a law requiring that every coin and bill minted or printed bear the words "In God We Trust."[39]

By that time—the middle of the twentieth century—most other nations of the world had followed the British and American example of using paper currency. The printing presses of the nations daily churned out millions of pieces of paper that had the force of legal tender. In light of how much money moves around the globe today and how often various currencies change hands, it is hard to imagine a system more effective than the printed bill. Without it, the peoples of the world might still have to carry pieces of gold and silver.

Printing paper currency may well be one of the most important business functions ever performed by the printing press. There are others as well, however.

Insurance policies. Bills of sale. Contracts. Memorandums. All these and more are issued each day by millions of companies around the globe. Each of these companies relies in some way either on a printing press or on its many descendants, which include the typewriter, fax machine, and personal computer.

Take contracts for example. Each day, businesses and individuals make thousands of contracts with each other for specific services at specific costs. Of course there were contracts before there were printing presses, but it was much more difficult to enforce those contracts because they were handwritten and could easily smudge and become difficult to read. The appearance of the printed page was doubtless a great improvement for the making and enforcing of business contracts.

In addition, there are now millions of items in certificate form that can only be produced with a specific form of printing. Stock certificates are embossed and engraved, as are some diplomas and licenses. The legibility and attractiveness of these documents is important.

By about 1964, the printing press in its various forms had become the instrument that allowed the Western world to regulate finances, establish patterns of commerce, and provide legality to contracts and documents. Much of the Third World was still left out of the loop, though, because the printing press and its descendants had not reached all parts of the globe. In 1964, an important book was published, a book that described how print media was about to go even farther than it already had. The book was Marshall McLuhan's *Understanding Media,*

The financial systems of countries and businesses rely heavily on the printing press. Not only is currency printed, but so are contracts and certificates of ownership, such as these stock certificates. The legal and financial power that these pieces of paper hold is enormous and vital to the conduct of international commerce.

and the processes that he predicted for the near future largely came true in the form of the personal computer. As one of the greatest and most powerful descendants of the printing press, the personal computer has changed our world.

10

Every Man His Own Printer:
The Personal Computer

Is the printing press still relevant today?

Not surprisingly, the answer is yes. Many of today's seemingly essential technologies—the computer, printer, fax machine, cell phone, and so on—are in some ways the descendants of the printing press. The standardization brought to the Western world by the use of the printing press led to the standardization that we experience today in synchronized clocks, computer printouts, and the like. Not only does the printing press remain relevant, it appears in the form of the personal computer and printer in the offices and homes of tens of millions of Americans, whether they work for IBM or are busily writing the Great American Novel at home.

The medium is the message.

—Marshall McLuhan,
Understanding Media, 1964

Printing seemed both precious and obsolete at the midpoint of the twentieth century. On one hand, more care was taken than ever before by writers, editors, proofreaders, and typesetters because the standard for publishing had risen to a very high level. This was the era of poets such as Robert Frost and Langston Hughes and prose writers such as John Steinbeck, Saul Bellow, and others. It was a remarkable time in the history of print culture.

At the same time, many of these esteemed poets and writers

believed that they were living in the last phase of the golden age of print. Television had appeared in the United States and was about to spread throughout Europe. Radio had been popular for nearly 40 years. There was a profound pessimism among educated people who loved the world of print; they feared that print's day was coming to an end. It would be replaced, they thought, by a fundamentally oral culture, in which what was said and heard on radio and television would dominate.

Then came a book by Marshall McLuhan. *Understanding Media: The Extensions of Man* was published in 1964. Critics at the time and ever since have hailed it as one of the truly influential books of the twentieth century, a landmark in understanding how print has come to permeate almost every aspect of American life—indeed, the life of all people living in the developed world. McLuhan's thesis is both extremely simple and surprisingly complex. It can be summed up in these words: "The medium is the message."[40]

McLuhan argued that since the time of Gutenberg, people living in the Western world had come increasingly under the spell of one type of truth: that which is printed. He admitted that the creation of radio and television had presented new packages of reality for the Western information consumer, but more important, he argued that consumers do not know what they are "buying" or "sampling." Consumers think they are buying a book and reading a mystery story, buying a magazine and reading about a celebrity, turning on the radio and listening to the news, or turning on the television and watching a comedy. But in fact, McLuhan argued, the consumer is buying or sampling the medium itself: that the medium is the product.

McLuhan made some fascinating comparisons between what he called "hot" and "cool" media. "Hot" items, such as television and billboards, leave little work to be done by the consumer; they are nonparticipatory. "Cool" technologies such as the telephone and radio leave a good deal of information to be "completed" by the recipient. Print materials clearly fall into

Marshall McLuhan, author of the landmark *Understanding Media: The Extensions of Man,* stated that "The medium is the message." Published in 1964, McLuhan's book explored how the printed word had changed society since Gutenberg's time and the implications of those changes.

the "cool" media category since reading involves the participation of the person who reads.

McLuhan did not use the following analogy; it comes from recent American folklore.

A very skillful customs inspector has worked on a border, let's say the U.S.–Canadian border, for many years. This inspector is credited with having a "nose" for detecting smugglers and their goods. Although he has caught many smugglers, one man has frustrated him for years. At least once and sometimes twice a month, this man would drive up to the inspection point in a large trailer truck. The inspector always thoroughly searched the vehicle and its contents and grilled the driver, but to no avail. One day when the driver pulls up, the inspector tells him that he is retiring, and that, as a professional courtesy, he would be thrilled to know what it is that this particular man (who he can tell is a smuggler) has been smuggling all these years.

The driver grins and replies: "Oh, that's easy. Trucks."

Because the customs inspector was so focused on the contents of the trucks, he failed to pay enough attention to the vehicles themselves. This, McLuhan would argue, is what we do with the media and the information they bring: we focus on the content and neglect to observe the media itself, which has become a self-perpetuating message.

McLuhan died in 1980, just as the computer revolution was about to kick off. We can only imagine what he might have thought of the personal computer, which was the next logical step in the development of the printing press.

In addition to McLuhan's influential work, two revolutions, one social and one technical, that occurred between 1960 and 1980 changed the way many Westerners felt about the printed word.

The first was the Youth Rebellion of the 1960s. Beginning in around 1964 with the Free Speech Movement at the University of California at Berkeley, thousands of young Americans began demanding greater openness in their society. Young people demonstrated against American intervention in Vietnam and against the hierarchical establishment in the universities and corporations. To their parents, the young students appeared ungrateful for all that American society had provided them.

The youth movement took place in Europe as well. Student

demonstrations in Paris in 1968 helped bring down the government of President Charles de Gaulle. Meanwhile, the youth protest movement in the United States became so large that people spoke of a "generation gap" between parents (who had come of age during World War II) and children (who had been born soon after the war ended).

The youth movement disdained most traditional education. Classics such as the poems of Shakespeare, Cervantes, and even Mark Twain were seen as hopelessly "classist" and sometimes

Romance Novels

Most novels of the nineteenth century emphasized male heroes and masculine themes. But soon after the turn of the twentieth century, publishers began to gear much of their material to women readers.

The British firm of Mills & Boon, founded in 1907, started the trend. Mills & Boon began as a general publisher, but by the time World War II ended, Mills & Boon were making most of their money from novels that featured women in all sorts of situations: some of the characters were fierce and heroic, others were shy and retiring. The firm became better known than its authors, and advertisements urged British women to ask their local librarian for "A Mills & Boon, if you please."

Mills & Boon merged with the Canadian publisher Harlequin in 1971. From then on, the two firms went from strong to stunningly successful. In 1998, Mills, Boon and Harlequin published more than 200 paperback novels, which were translated into 24 languages and sold in 100 countries. In the home islands of the United Kingdom, Mills & Boon had over 11 million loyal readers. No other publishing company, from the time of Erasmus and Sir Thomas More to the present, can boast such sales.

Though it does not fall into the romance novel category, the Harry Potter books also originated in the United Kingdom, and also involve a successful woman. The author, a single mother, wrote her original stories in the shelter of friendly coffeehouses. The books have now sold over 100 million copies, making J. K. Rowling perhaps the single most successful author of all time. Harry Potter books may eventually outsell the Old and New Testaments.

even racist. The great tomes of Western literature, which had been accumulating since the time of Johannes Gutenberg, were now seen as irrelevant at best, and dangerous at worst. Young people reminded one another not to trust "anyone over 30."

A whole new cottage industry of alternative publications began to appear. *Mother Jones* had been around for some time, as had the *Catholic Daily Worker*. But now there appeared *Rolling Stone Magazine, Playboy, Utne Reader*, and numerous other journals and magazines. As a whole, these new publications spoke to the desire of young Americans for a more idealistic and less materialistic society.

American involvement in the Vietnam War ended in 1975. The election of Ronald Reagan as the 40th President in 1980 appeared to herald a return to traditional American values, as represented in magazines such as *Time, Newsweek*, and *U.S. News & World Report*. And then, just as Reagan's administration got under way, came a second revolution.

It was the personal computer.

Computers first appeared in the laboratories of the U.S. government. They were bulky, even enormous machines that took a long time to perform their tasks, but when they were finished with a task, their chance of being mathematically correct was startlingly high, better than 99 percent. The American public had its first good look at a computer in the movie *2001: A Space Odyssey*, which featured a computer named HAL that performed calculations for a crew in outer space. Americans were both delighted and disturbed by the movie, but few guessed that such a device would make its way onto their desks within less than two decades.

The personal computer was pioneered by the engineers of Apple Computer in California. The engineers had their first model ready in 1976, and the first computers began to appear in American homes over the next few years. Although these machines were a great deal smaller than the giants that existed in government offices, the early personal computer shared an annoying tendency with its forebears: it was maddeningly slow. Even under the best circumstances, the American consumer spent hours typing commands and then waiting for long periods of time as the computer responded to those commands. Until about 1985, it seemed as if computers were doomed to live a shadow life among programmers, engineers, and government agency workers.

However, in conjunction with the release of the 386 processor chip in 1986, the first fast, highly responsive personal computers began to be sold. Then the World Wide Web caught the attention of the public in the mid-1990s; suddenly the American consumer had access to billions of bytes of information that previously had been available only to people working at the Pentagon.

No innovation since Gutenberg's first use of movable type had been a comparable agent of change. At the same time, the computer threatened to both undo traditional American life and enhance the possibilities of that life.

Two companies, Macintosh and Microsoft, led the way. International Business Machines (IBM) sanctioned and used Microsoft's software, whereas Macintosh delighted in its iconoclastic approach to the business. Both companies produced personal computers for the consumer marketplace. And Americans bought them.

And bought them. And bought them. Between 1980 and 2000, a true revolution occurred in American life. With the invention of the World Wide Web by Tim Berners-Lee in 1990, Americans gradually came to use their computers to shop, learn, connect, and communicate, and suddenly the old telephone ad that said "reach out and touch someone" seemed obsolete. Now you could reach out and touch the world just by moving your fingers on a plastic keyboard.

The computer also showed the potential to bridge the "communication gap" between parents and children, whether they were in their 20s, 40s, or older. Although young people were

The personal computer, the cause of the most recent revolution in the history of printing, began to appear in increasing numbers of business offices and academic institutions in the 1980s. With the advent of the Internet and the World Wide Web in 1990, the way in which information and ideas are communicated once again changed forever.

the first to become truly excited about the computer and its potential for interaction, older Americans bought computers in great numbers and then used them to participate in what was soon called the "New Global Economy."

One question emerged: Had the computer made the printed word obsolete?

During the mid-1990s, many social critics answered in the affirmative. They pointed out that Gutenberg's invention had led to the replacement of scribes by printers, and that the computer revolution would lead to the end of the making of books. But the predictions of death were premature.

What the United States, most of Europe, and many other parts of the world experienced was a return to literacy, but a new type of "hyperliteracy" that involved much more movement and selection than careful reading. Even so, the continued emphasis on literacy meant that books retained their place in scholarship. In fact, books on how to use computers appeared everywhere.

Today, there are more books in the world than ever before. In the United States alone, roughly 60,000 new titles are registered with the U.S. Library of Congress each year. This number does not include the thousands of books that are printed by family members for their relations or by small presses that are not concerned with copyright, or the millions of stories that are written and circulated on the Web every year. We, the people of the civilized world, are more awash in print than at any other time in existence.

The printing press, whether it is Gutenberg's original, Mergenthaler's Linotype, or the swift printing machines attached to personal computers today, has had a profound influence on the development of the modern world. Imagine for a moment that most of the other elements of modern life are present, but that the press and all its descendants are not. Just think:

- A computer could calculate the total of a grocery bill, but the bill would have to be handwritten.

- Adding machines could come up with the answers to complex calculations, but the results could not be printed out.

- Contracts could be made and witnessed to, but it would be more difficult to enforce them, since writing them in longhand might lead to questions of authenticity and meaning.

And so on. The world would not be the same.

Many of the other conveniences of modern life probably would not exist today had the printing press not been developed. It is difficult to imagine libraries and bookstores without printed volumes, or even train stations and bus depots without printed advertisements of departure times.

For all the remarkable advances of modern times—from the telephone to the radio to the automobile—we have to thank Johannes Gutenberg and all the others involved in the development of the printing press. From its earliest beginnings in Mainz, Germany, to the rapid printing of *The New York Times* today, the printing press has profoundly altered the world in which we live.

3000 B.C.	Writing begins in Egypt and Mesopotamia
2500 B.C.	Writing begins in Pakistan
800–600 B.C.	Greeks adopt and alter the Phoenician (phonetic) alphabet
200 B.C.– **A.D.400**	Height of Roman Empire; use of the Latin alphabet
450–600	The Dark Ages in Europe
775–850	The Carolingian Renaissance in Europe; minuscule (lowercase) letters begin to be used
868	The first book printed in China, the *Diamond Sutra*
1040	Pi Sheng uses movable type in China
1100–1300	Paper begins to arrive in Europe, allowing for expansion of writing
1446	The Korean king decrees use of new 25-letter alphabet
1450s	Johannes Gutenberg uses movable type in Mainz, Germany; his Bible is the first to be printed
1460–1500	Printing spreads across Europe
1500	By this year, about 8 million books have been printed
1517	Martin Luther issues the Ninety-Five Theses; Hans Lufft quickly prints and circulates them
1522	Luther publishes the Bible in German
1525	William Tyndale publishes the New Testament in English
1532	Antonio Blado prints Machiavelli's *The Prince*
1533	John Calvin's *The Institutes of the Christian Religion* is published
1542	Johannes Oporinus prints the Koran in Switzerland
1543	Copernicus's and Vesalius's books are published
1550s	First printing press established in Moscow
1559	The *Index of Prohibited Books* is established by the Roman Catholic Church
1611	Galileo's *The Starry Messenger* is published
1611	Robert Barker prints the King James Bible in London
1631	The "Wicked Bible" comes out in England
1661	Rev. John Eliot publishes the Bible in Algonquin
1687	Joseph Streater prints Isaac Newton's *Mathematical Principles of Natural Philosophy*

1690	Elizabeth Holt prints John Locke's *An Essay Concerning Human Understanding*
1690	The first American newspaper is printed in Boston
1690	The first American paper money is printed in Boston
1696	Anonymous author publishes *An Essay in Defence of the Female Sex*
1719	Daniel Defoe's *Robinson Crusoe* is published in England
1733	Benjamin Franklin publishes the first *Poor Richard's Almanack*
1735	Trial of John Peter Zenger in New York City
1751	The first volume of Diderot and d'Alembert's *Encylopédie* is published
1755	William Strahan prints Samuel Johnson's *Dictionary of the English Language*
1771	Louis-Sebastien Mercier publishes *The Year 2440* in France
1776	William Strahan prints Edward Gibbon's *History of the Decline and Fall of the Roman Empire*
1776	John Dunlap prints the Declaration of Independence
1791	Joseph Johnson prints Thomas Paine's *The Rights of Man*
1792	Johnson prints Mary Wollstonecraft's *A Vindication of the Rights of Woman*
1797	Thomas Spence publishes *The Rights of Infants*
1798	Trial of Joseph Johnson in England
1807	William Wilberforce publishes antislavery tract
1852	Harriet Beecher Stowe's *Uncle Tom's Cabin* is published
1857	Florence Nightingale publishes *Notes on Matters Affecting the Health, Efficiency, and Hospital Administration of the British Army*
1859	Charles Darwin publishes *On the Origin of Species*
1860	John Mill publishes *On Liberty*
1863	Jules Verne writes about Paris in the years 1960 and 1961
1868	The typewriter is patented in the United States
1880s	The Linotype machine appears
1907	Mills & Boon is formed in Britain, beginning the romance novel industry
1923	*Time* magazine published for first time

1920s The radio appears in American homes

1950s The television appears in American homes

1964 Marshall McLuhan publishes *Understanding Media*

1980 Personal computers begin to appear in American homes

2000 Total number of new books published annually in the United States nears 60,000

Chapter 2: Early Printing: China, Japan, Korea, and Germany

1 Daniel J. Boorstin, *The Discoverers*. New York: Random House, 1983, 499.

2 Ibid., 500.

3 Ibid., 506–507.

Chapter 3: Printing and Language: The Use of the Vernacular

4 Melissa Conway, *The Diario of the Printing Press of San Jacopo di Ripoli, Commentary and Transcription*. Florence, Italy: Leo S. Olschki, 1999.

5 S. H. Steinberg, *Five Hundred Years of Printing*. New York: Penguin Books, 1955, 90.

6 John Clyde Oswald, *A History of Printing*. New York: D. Appleton, 1928, 154.

7 Stewart Robb, *Nostradamus on Napoleon, Hitler and the Present Crisis*. Scribners, 1941, 5–6.

8 Ibid., 168.

9 Ibid., 184.

10 John Carter and Percy H. Muir, eds., *Printing and the Mind of Man: The Impact of Print on Five Centuries of Western Civilization*. New York: Holt, Rinehart & Winston, 1967, 33.

Chapter 4: Printing and the Religious Revolution

11 Martin Luther, *Ninety-Five Theses*. R. S. Grignon, trans. New York: Bartleby.com, 2001. <http://www.bartleby.com/36/4/1.html>

12 Steinberg, *Five Hundred Years*, 103.

13 Sir Sidney Lee and Sir Stephen Leslie, *Dictionary of National Biography, Vol. 57*. London: 1898, 428.

14 Steinberg, *Five Hundred Years*, 53.

Chapter 5: Printing and the Scientific Revolution

15 Quoted in George Schwartz and Philip W. Bishop, eds., *Moments of Discovery: The Origins of Science*. New York: Basic Books, 1958, 220.

16 Ibid., 231.

17 Carter and Muir, *Printing and the Mind of Man*, 43.

18 Carter and Muir, *Printing and the Mind of Man*, p. 76.

Chapter 6: Early American Printing

19 Douglas C. McMurtrie, *The Book* Oxford: Oxford University Press, 1943, 390–392.

20 Calvin P. Otto, *Publick Occurrences, Both Foreign and Domestic: The First American Newspaper*. Bennington, VT: Americana Classics, 1975, 13.

21 Robert F. Roden, *The Cambridge Press, 1638-1692*. New York: Dodd, Mead, 1903, 86.

22 Benjamin Franklin, *Poor Richard's Almanacks, Illustrated by Norman Rockwell*. New York: Ballantine Books, 1977, 3.

23 Nancy Sirkis, *Reflections of 1776: The Colonies Revisited*. New York: Viking Press, 1974, 116.

24 Frederick R. Goff, *The John Dunlap Broadside: The First Printing of the Declaration of Independence*. Washington, D.C.: Library of Congress, 1976, 4–12.

25 William M. Vanderweyde, editor, *The Selected Works of Thomas Paine*. (New York: The Thomas Paine National Historical Association, 1925) volume II, 263–264

Chapter 7: The Enlightenment: Edinburgh, London, and Paris

26 Judith Drake, *An Essay in Defence of the Female Sex. In which are inserted the characters of a pedant, a vertuoso, a squire, a poetaster, a beau, a city-critick, &c. in a letter to a lady. Written by a lady*. London, 1696, 87–89.

27 Roy Porter, *The Creation of the Modern World: The Untold Story of the British Enlightenment*. New York: W. W. Norton, 2000, 73.

28 Ibid., 73.

29 Quoted in Smith, George, *Dictionary of National Biography, Vol. 55*. London, 1898, 18.

30 Robert Darnton, *The Forbidden Best-Sellers of Pre-Revolutionary France*. New York: W. W. Norton, 1995, 300–310.

31 Ibid., 133.

32 Ibid., 133–134.

Chapter 8: The Press and Human Freedom

33 Gerald P. Tyson, *Joseph Johnson: A Liberal Publisher*. Iowa City: University of Iowa Press, 1979, 136–175.

34 Carter and Muir, *Printing and the Mind of Man*, 198.

35 Mergenthaler Linotype Company, *Linotype: Its Construction and Working Explained*. New York: Mergenthaler Linotype Company, 1895, 1–2.

Chapter 9: Printing and the Financial Revolution

36 Henry Yule, ed., *The Book of Ser Marco Polo, The Venetian, 2 vols.* London, 1875, 409–410.

37 Alice Lounsberry, *Treasure Fisherman: Sir William Phips.* New York: Scribners, 1941, p. 232.

38 Joseph B. Felt, *An Historical Account of Massachusetts Currency.* Boston: Perkins & Marvin, 1839, 50.

39 John A. Garraty and Mark C. Carnes, eds., *American National Biography, Vol. 4.* Oxford: Oxford University Press, 1999, 741.

Chapter 10: Every Man His Own Printer: The Personal Computer

40 Marshall McLuhan, *Understanding Media: The Extensions of Man.* New York: McGraw-Hill, 1964, 13.

Adkins, Nelson F., ed. *Thomas Paine: Common Sense and Other Political Writings.* New York: Liberal Arts Press, 1953.

Bobrick, Benson. *Wide as the Waters: The Story of the English Bible and the Revolution It Inspired.* New York: Simon and Schuster, 2001.

Boorstin, Daniel J. *The Discoverers.* New York: Random House, 1983.

Carter, John, and Percy H. Muir, eds. *Printing and the Mind of Man: The Impact of Print on Five Centuries of Western Civilization.* New York: Holt, Rinehart & Winston, 1967.

Conway, Melissa. *The Diario of the Printing Press of San Jacopo di Ripoli, Commentary and Transcription.* Florence, Italy: Leo S. Olschki, 1999.

Darnton, Robert. *The Forbidden Best-Sellers of Pre-Revolutionary France.* New York: W. W. Norton, 1995.

Eisenstein, Elizabeth L. *The Printing Revolution in Early Modern Europe.* Cambridge: Cambridge University Press, 1983.

Goff, Frederick R. *The John Dunlap Broadside: The First Printing of the Declaration of Independence.* Washington, D.C.: Library of Congress, 1976.

Goldstone, Lawrence, and Nancy Goldstone. *Out of the Flames: The Remarkable Story of a Fearless Scholar, a Fatal Heresy, and One of the Rarest Books in the World.* New York: Broadway Books, 2002.

Locke, John. *An Essay Concerning Human Understanding.* London, 1690.

Lull, Timothy F., ed. *Martin Luther's Basic Theological Writings.* Minneapolis, Minn.: Fortress Press, 1989.

McLuhan, Marshall. *Understanding Media: The Extensions of Man,* New York: McGraw-Hill, 1964.

McMurtrie, Douglas C. *The Book: The Story of Printing & Bookmaking.* Oxford: Oxford University Press, 1943.

Mergenthaler Linotype Company. *Linotype: Its Construction and Working Explained.* New York: Mergenthaler Linotype Company, 1895.

More, Thomas. *Utopia and a Dialogue of Comfort Against Tribulation.* London: Everyman's Library, 1910.

Nussbaum, Arthur. *A History of the Dollar.* New York: Columbia University Press, 1957.

Painter, George D. *William Caxton: A Biography.* New York: G. P. Putnam's Sons, 1977.

Palmer, Samuel. *A General History of Printing, from Its First Invention in the City of Mentz, to Its First Progress and Propagation through the Most Celebrated Cities in Europe.* London, 1732.

Porter, Roy. *The Creation of the Modern World: The Untold Story of the British Enlightenment.* New York: W. W. Norton, 2000.

Robb, Stewart. *Nostradamus on Napoleon, Hitler and the Present Crisis.* New York: Scribners, 1941.

Schwartz, George, and Philip W. Bishop, eds. *Moments of Discovery: The Origins of Science.* New York: Basic Books, 1958.

Sirkis, Nancy. *Reflections of 1776: The Colonies Revisited.* New York: Viking Press, 1974.

Smith, George. *Dictionary of National Biography.* Leslie Stephen and Sidney Lee, eds. London: 1898.

Steinberg, S. H. *Five Hundred Years of Printing.* New York: Penguin Books, 1955.

Thulin, Oskar. *A Life of Luther.* Philadelphia: Fortress Press, 1966.

Twitchett, Denis. *Printing and Publishing in Medieval China.* New York: Frederic C. Beil, 1983.

Tyson, Gerald P. *Joseph Johnson: A Liberal Publisher.* Iowa City: University of Iowa Press, 1979.

Verne, Jules. *The Lost Novel: Paris in the Twentieth Century.* Translated by Richard Howard. New York: Random House, 1996.

Winterich, John T. *Early American Books & Printing.* New York: Houghton Mifflin, 1935.

Boorstin, Daniel J. *The Discoverers.* New York: Random House, 1983.

Eisenstein, Elizabeth L. *The Printing Revolution in Early Modern Europe.* Cambridge: Cambridge University Press, 1983.

Goldstone, Lawrence, and Nancy Goldstone. *Out of the Flames: The Remarkable Story of a Fearless Scholar, a Fatal Heresy, and One of the Rarest Books in the World.* New York: Broadway Books, 2002.

McLuhan, Marshall. *Understanding Media: The Extensions of Man.* New York: McGraw-Hill, 1964.

Steinberg, S. H. *Five Hundred Years of Printing.* New York: Penguin Books, 1955.

WEBSITES

Benjamin Franklin and His Printing Press
http://sln.fi.edu/franklin/printer/printer.html

The British Library: The Diamond Sutra
http://www.bl.uk/collections/treasures/diamond.html

The Glory of Chinese Printing
http://www.cgan.com/english/english/cpg/indexen.htm

Gutenberg's Invention
http://www.gutenberg.de/english/erfindun.htm

History of Books and Printing
http://www.nypl.org/research/chss/grd/resguides/bookhist.html

Invention of the Printing Press
http://www.ideafinder.com/history/inventions/story039.htm

Johannes Gutenberg and the Printing Press
http://inventors.about.com/library/inventors/blJohannesGutenberg.htm

Renaissance: Printing and Thinking
http://www.learner.org/exhibits/renaissance/printing.html

Trinity College: Book of Kells
http://www.tcd.ie/Library/kells.htm

Virtual Museum Printing-Press
http://www.imultimedia.pt/museuvirtpress/index_i.html

Samuel Willard Crompton is a historian and biographer who lives in western Massachusetts. He is the author or editor of more than 20 books, with titles ranging from *100 Spiritual Leaders Who Shaped World History* to *The Ultimate Book of Lighthouses.* He is a major contributor to *American National Biography,* published by Oxford University Press. Crompton teaches both Western civilization and American history at Holyoke Community College. He has written extensively for Chelsea House, including *Waterloo, Pakistan,* and *Alexander the Great.*

ABOUT THE AUTHOR